Couplings and Groupings

MEGAN TERRY
Couplings and Groupings

PANTHEON BOOKS

A DIVISION OF RANDOM HOUSE, NEW YORK

Library of Congress Cataloging in Publication Data
Terry, Megan.   Couplings and Groupings.
1. Sex Customs—United States. 2. Interpersonal
relations. 3. Marriage—United States. I. Title.
HQ18.U5T47   301.41'7973   72-3418
ISBN 0-394-47109-1

Manufactured in the United States of America
by American Book-Stratford Press, New York

First Edition

Dedicated to:

my mother		my father
my stepfather		my stepmother
my stepsister	my sister	my half-sister
my stepbrother	her children	her children
their children	my aunts	
	my uncles	
	my cousins	
	their children	

Preface

When I was asked to do a book—a report on changing attitudes toward traditional marriage in America—I was delighted. People have been my life's study. As preparation for my work as a playwright, I spend most of my time talking with people. I've also been very fortunate lately, because in connection with my theater work I've been able to tour the planet twice in the last four years.

I started this book before the women's liberation movement had made such a strong impact, and I was beginning to think of settling down and perhaps even getting legally married. In fact the traditional pressures were growing so heavy I began to have pictures in my mind of all the grandchildren I would be presenting to my mother.

But I was saved. Saved by doing this book and saved by the political thinking of the women's movement. I'm not going to get legally married, but I still think I'll have one or two children, and raise them the way I think a child should be raised, in the theater.

Before I started the interview process, I thought that I'd find lots of Americans, the younger ones, living the way I'd been living since I was sixteen: on my own, going with the moment, staying as long as love lasted and then moving on. Many of the big headline stories in the media seemed to indicate that the sexual revolution had freed women, and the youth culture had freed children. Well,

it ain't necessarily so. On the surface people are strug-
gling to create new forms of emotional relationships, but
they are still plagued with the old problems. Organized
religion seems to still have a stronger hold on Americans
than I had realized. People I interviewed who came from
strong religious backgrounds appear to be making what
look like very good choices for new ways of living in
couples or groups.

Work on this book has led me to speculate that the
new "experiments in living" represent a revolt against
the isolation of the machine age: some people are being
driven to closer, more tribal relationships in retaliation
against the machined isolation. But it must be acknowl-
edged that this terrible "machine," in tearing up old family patterns, has also relieved individuals from having to
stay stuck in old family vices. With the mobility provided by the auto one may simply drive away.

Many people have discovered they can make different things happen to their heads and bodies by attaching
themselves to various other bundles of memories, experiences, and vibrations. Through serial marriage, or multiple
love relationships, people can now live many emotional
lives. Carnal knowledge can indeed contribute to one's
growth as an individual. A person can grow through
sexual experience if his attitudes are expansive, but he
can crash and crack up if they are not, if he worries
about "What will the neighbors say?"

People are more and more frequently "coupling" or
pairing to try each other out before legal marriage. People of the same sex form couples and "play house" like
legally married heterosexuals. People are "grouping," in
extended families, communes, sub-cultures, underground
and over-ground religious organizations and political
groups. These "new" ways of coupling and grouping

are really traditional American explorations. The American has always been looking for "new territory," and a faster, cheaper way to get there. If what you've got isn't working, move out, "move ahead," try something or *someone* else.

Some who hoped for political apocalypse in the 1960's have turned inward to look for themselves, or battened down in nests with one or several others to find fulfillment in inter-personal relationships. Some people seem to be trying to work toward "happiness," others are fighting a holding action. In the richest country in the world many people have the time and the money to experiment on their families, or their concepts of family, their bodies, their souls: they have time to choose which spices shall sit on their kitchen shelves, and to pick from a rainbow of possibilities just how they'll have that orgasm this afternoon.

No one, no matter how many people one knows, or how many one may interview for a book like this, can hope to do any sort of definitive work on how people are living emotionally with each other in the United States these days. What follows is a small selection from some rich and intense conversations I've had with a number of vital Americans. The people I talked with tell in their own words of their lives, their thoughts, their experiences. Pseudonyms, false places of residence, fictitious jobs, have been created for them to protect the innocent, to avoid family fights and needless embarrassment. I wish all the two hundred people I interviewed were included here, but then the book couldn't have been portable. I want to think everyone who helped me put this book together. My debt to them is endless and evolving, because I personally changed so much as the book progressed. I've profited from the examples and advice of my fellows. I want to thank you for the good times, your openness, and the deep closeness we shared on many, many occasions.

M.T.

Omaha, Nebraska, 1972

In this world all men are strangers—uprooted.

—Simone Weil

Couplings and Groupings

GEORGE ALMQUIST is a teamster, fifty-three years old. George and I have gone fishing together many, many times. He taught me to play pool, shuffleboard, and blackjack. I try to see him every time I go home to the Northwest. He always lays what he thinks right out on the line.

Listen, I think to get married you should marry someone of the opposite sex. The first thing you need is money. Love? Love is the next best thing to help you get along if you get married, but what you really need is money.

Used to be in the old days the college kids weren't married, and if they were they kept it quiet. Now about forty percent of them are married and they don't keep it quiet. He marries some gal and she puts him through school doing the ironing and such, and he gets his degree, then he boots his family out and he starts raising whiskers.

The only friends I had who were happily married are divorced now. They had so much fun that they couldn't stand it. So they got divorced and then they got remarried. I think the only true love is the people that are married about six months. After that, true love goes out the window. Something else enters, and it ain't the White Dove. It's generally the milkman or something like that. My parents were happily married because there was no beer parlors in those days. The old man was out digging and grubbing, and the old woman was washing clothes and canning and there was no time for extracurricular activities. The only time they had fun was in the evening by the moonlight; consequently we had a big family. Every nine months somebody was born. I lay it all on the fact that we didn't have TV in those days. Up to about 1935 my brothers and sisters were happy too, but then they got radios, and Bingo! Even my brothers would sit up all night long trying to get different stations around the country. Consequently the women were left frustrated.

Then the kids were two years apart. Now they got TV the kids are three years apart. And if they invent enough more stuff you can forget about taking birth control pills. Ah, hell, women haven't got enough sense to stay home and take care of the family any more, they got to get a job. So they go out and get a job on a different shift from the old man. Now the old man comes home and turns on the TV till he can't stand it any more and he goes to bed. The old lady comes home and she's already taken the pill and she watches that TV till about six o'clock in the morning, well, she's wasted the pill.

So it's my personal opinion that these guys who put these pills out are taking the public. Do away with TV or the pill! This guy who drives with me, his only complaint about marriage is that his wife leaves him sleeping in the big chair till six o'clock in the morning when he comes home drunk. This other guy in my crew, his wife makes him sleep in the basement, but his only complaint is there's no bathtub down there. She locks the door on him because he only comes home on Monday, Tuesday, and Sunday.

Most of the guys I work with love their wives, but they can't stand them 'cause they're married to them. The old man goes out and he does wrong, he comes home and confesses. The first thing these women do is go out and tell the whole neighborhood what her old man has done. So now, the old man can't trust her, see? You see, after a man's been married to a certain woman for a number of years he kinda looks up to her with a mother complex. And don't forget, if you ever get married and the guy comes home and says, How ya doin', Mother—you hit him right in the puss.

DOROTHY BREWSTER is a successful writer with more than forty-five cookbooks to her credit. She is forty-two and lives on a beautiful ranch in New Mexico. She's fixed up one of the barns for her test kitchen and another as a writing studio. Dorothy loves to be in love and she's been in love with some men and many women.

I suppose I'm so strong because my father was a child beater. In a family, if you beat a boy up, that will make him weak, if you beat a girl up, that will make her very strong. The battered child syndrome. My father was given to physical violence, would beat the kids up when he was tired, and he wasn't an Irishman who was drunk, you know. He was just a middle-class man who came home at the end of a day and beat up the kids.

My grandfather had the biggest house in town. I know my father very well, and I really like him. He was a very intellectual man—I mean, you don't have to be stupid to be violent. I think my mother enjoyed it. I think she sometimes instigated it. He would come home at six o'clock for dinner, and at the dinner table she would say everything we did wrong all day, knowing that he was at the boiling point. He would just blow his top. It didn't make him a villain to me because I loved him, but it certainly deflated my brother, who was the alleged male in the family. The little brother wasn't born then and when he was, Father never touched him, which was interesting.

The little brother was fourteen years younger and he never was raised by my father. My older brother became a fortune pilot, I became a writer of cookbooks, and my little brother became an accountant. So maybe violence is necessary.

I've always wanted a son—I never wanted a daughter. Now I am thankful I don't have them. I think they would be a tremendous burden to the only thing I do well—and that's writing.

My cats take orders, you know. They come to my typewriter a lot and then go away for another hour—imagine a baby crying! You don't accept responsibilities in life that you aren't emotionally up to—your own mind protects you. I've never been married—I used to live with guys, but I never married. I used to tell all gay girls I was married because it would seem to capture their fancy. I made them feel they really weren't with somebody as queer as they were. And then I think I started to believe it. I didn't make any of the guys up, but I never married any of them.

There've been a lot of guys—one when I was in Vermont. My first guy was when I was in high school. The guy I used to say I was married to—I met in Vermont and I waitressed and he waitered all summer, and we lived together. We pretended to everyone we were married, because it was cheaper. I think we dug each other, but I don't really think we dug sex. I think we did sex, we certainly made it, but you know, when you talk to somebody their memory is in retrospect, and the past improves, so it comes out the way you want it. If I were to believe we really enjoyed sex, I would have to believe that I have tremendously more of a heterosexual capacity than I do. And I would wonder what went wrong. And so in retrospect I would say we didn't enjoy sex.

I've slept with men—the problem isn't sleeping with them, the problem is appreciating them, and being able to live with a man. If a person by the age of thirty-seven hasn't been able to live with a man or woman, then there is something vitally wrong. I'm not talking about staying with each other. I don't think it's suspect in any way idealistically, emotionally, sexually, etc., if you live a year with somebody, a year with somebody else, two years with somebody else, five years with somebody else, I think it's suspect if you don't make the attempt to live with somebody at all. Suspect, not as a human being, but as somebody who feels *anything*. How can you avoid it, if you feel something?

I think of dwarfs, crazy people, or freaks—*somebody* always finds *somebody*. If you don't ever find somebody where you say—let's live together, let's have a home—I think if you never have that experience, I think if you're thirty and you don't have that experience, that's very strange.

Anyone can get married, anyone can have children. The enigma to me is, who *is* this person who can't and won't live with someone? It's never happened to me. As early as I was formed, I wanted to live with somebody. I used to say I wanted to get married, but now certain things have happened where I think it's emotionally impossible. When I was young, I didn't care what kind of a job anybody had, or what they did around the house in terms of whether they picked up after themselves, or if they read the *Los Angeles Times* every day, or if they didn't fit in with the few friends I've maintained through the years—I didn't care. *Now*, I care, because I'm already formed. And well formed. Now I care—it's almost static—about what I want.

I was talking with a homosexual the other day who said, What do you do for a sex life—do you masturbate? And I said, Of course that's what I do. I masturbate. So she said, Oh, my God, you masturbate! I said, This is a nice turn of fate—the homosexuals of the world will turn against the masturbators. I mean, you know—the heterosexuals turn against the homosexuals and the homosexuals turn against the masturbators—the masturbators are then left to turn against the people they suspect have no sex at all. Let's all be intolerant of everybody, you know. And be proud of what we're able to accomplish but be completely intolerant of what anybody else is able to accomplish. That's what it comes down to.

You know the French expression, that sexual intercourse is a poor substitute for masturbation. In fantasy life you can choose anyone. I could choose Jacqueline Kennedy. Now could I do that going into a bar? Sometimes I choose men, sometimes mayors, black ones—it depends on the day. You could have a very powerful man, or you could have a symbol like a Negro, dark and forbidden, raping. As to women, I come up an awful lot in my own fantasies, I mean I'm there and some man is there. Most of my own fantasies are with men. And if I'm with a woman, then it's a man doing something to that woman. If I'm very attracted to a woman and am having a sex life with a woman, I guess my masturbation fantasies, which are always supplementary to my sex life, would be a man doing something to that woman.

I have a friend who is a psychoanalyst and she said, Tell me your masturbation fantasies and I'll tell you about yourself.

One night I got a whole room full of people and I got them all to tell their masturbation fantasies, and my girl at the time went to bed. She was disgusted at this conversation. But there was one girl in the room, she worked for *Time* Magazine, and she's a copy editor—I don't know what a copy editor is, but they're never supposed to get involved in the story, they look for mistakes —so we came around the room and everybody had said what their masturbation fantasies were, and they were wild. We were all drunk, and we came to Ann who's a copy editor, who said, You mean you really *think* of something? She said, I just *do* it. She masturbates thinking of nothing at all.

I *decided* to become a writer. I *didn't* decide to become a homosexual. I don't know how I became a homosexual.

When I was in boarding school, I had the sense that I was doing something wrong—it started one night with a back rub, the way everything starts. We were going to have a vocabulary test and I was rubbing a friend's back and we were giving each other words, and finally we came to the word "specious"—I remember this very well—and I said, Specious, and she said, Artificial, superficial, and I said, Use it in a sentence, and she said, I would be specious if I were to say I wouldn't want to turn over right now, and let your hands do exactly what they're doing. That's how we started. But I was fourteen and I never forgot it. And she turned over. And that's how it began. I loved her too, a lot. I never knew what happened to her.

We all are what we are, I don't know why we are what we are, but here we are. What's important is that we accommodate ourselves as gracefully as we can with who we are and never mind why. *Why* is a blame. I'm not going to blame my mother and father, and then blame *their* mother and father.

I am a terrible person. I pick up everything. I've never had a lover that I didn't turn into in five minutes' time. I pick somebody, love them, and suddenly I pick up their gestures and start becoming them. Then *I'm* all lost. Next I pull myself out and look for somebody else. I never have met anybody I complemented or who complemented me—I wouldn't let them. The only one I ever met was another writer and it was very important for me to put her down. So I did it. At that time, I needed to win more than she did. She was already established and very competitive. I'm certain that I hurt her a lot. But I think I would put anyone down. I think basically that's my way of making love, I put people down. Right now, what I seek in another is a sense of humor and that she read the *Los Angeles Times* every day. That's the truth. And I like big breasts—36C for starters.

A man?—Now I think I would appreciate a man more when I'm too old to find anything but human wrecks. I don't want a young man, because a man is to lean on, and I don't want a kid leaning on me who's not a woman. If I want a man, I want to lean. He better not be a weak man. Fairness has nothing to do with me.

Basically, I'm more attracted to a woman sexually. There are a lot of reasons: women smell better to me. When I had a diaphragm on, I nearly gagged. It smelled of male semen—it really goes back to the basic motivations of why a woman becomes homosexual; another woman would adore that smell. Men usually smell much more than women—their skin isn't as good. And I don't care what you say, under their arms men don't shave, and perspiration clings—many women find that musky odor attractive, I don't. I don't like to linger with a man, and a man—any man that I've had, and I've had a great many male lovers—they don't linger a lot. I'm told by some women who love men that of course a man lingers, of course he takes his time, of course he does everything that I think he doesn't do. I compared with a French girl recently the sex and love experience—I was trying to find out something from her because the last woman I was with said I was crazy. I said even thinking about a woman I can feel some excitement, right to my finger-tips—and this woman said, You're crazy, you try to romanticize things. This French woman came, and had some drinks—she had just broken up with her husband, and she really loved him and missed him terribly and I said, Tell me something, when you loved him, did you feel it right to the ends of your fingertips? And she said, Oh, my God, yes. The Germans have a word for it, it's something like *Fingerspittzelheim,* and she said, Of course, everybody feels that, yes? She said, I wouldn't love a man I couldn't feel to my fingertips. He left her for a younger woman. She's beautiful, she really is. It was interesting to talk to the French woman and find out that everything I've heard so many women say that they've found in another woman could be found in a man. In other words, I came away feeling the males I had made love to were the wrong males. That my idea of heterosexuality was formed on my own bad experiences with men. Everything I said I had looked for in a woman, she had found in a man.

I've tested men, but I've tested women too. Testing yourself is not repeating yourself—and what I've done is repeat myself. I used to lay men as much as I laid women, but I don't do that any more, because they're harder to come by and unreliable. Men at the age of forty-two are usually married, or neurotic, or desperately lonely. I just had an experience with a straight man, and we got along very well—I really liked him—and what I really liked about him was his looks—he was beautiful. A friend of mine from New York who didn't know I was gay had given him my name and he called me up. I really liked seeing him, I really liked him—he's a funny guy, he doesn't drink and he doesn't smoke. The strangest thing about him was he couldn't express himself, but he writes things down—he copies poems and things, and he's a businessman. He's the vice-president of an advertising agency. He pulls these things out and he shows these things to me that mean how he feels. Some about me, some about everything. He's a marvelous character—he's a brilliant man, but he can't talk.

One of the marvelous things about falling in love is explaining yourself to somebody and going through the marvelous process of their explaining themselves to you. It's a narcissistic thing. I think straight people do that too, but they don't have as many opportunities. I just know they don't. I mean, all the times I've lain in bed with a cigarette in a dark room and said, It's funny, my mother used to sing that song too, and the other person would say, Really? What was she like? And then you start.

Nobody is totally gay. I'm going to mention a woman now, and it's going to explain something. I'll call her Marian for now. She's a very wealthy woman. I happened to have an affair with her when she was in a very lonely period on her third millionaire. She was really unhappy and he was really unhappy and he was an old man, an awful man. She had no sex life, and she got involved with me when she wanted to write a book about him. She hired me as a ghostwriter, and we became very involved and very loving.

Then she met her present husband. She had an affair with him and then she married him, and she's married to him now. One night they were all at a big, long dinner table at this fancy sit-down dinner in Houston. Somebody brought in this copy of the Daughters of Bilitis magazine called the *Ladder*, and they were passing it around, joking, and she said tears filled her eyes; she had to leave the room. Because she knew she wasn't gay, but she had been in bed with me and made love to me and she understood that this isn't a freaky thing that people should be passing around the room. All these wealthy, privileged, millionaire-type people, unhappy themselves in their own ways, for compensation were passing this magazine around. Yet, she said, it had been such a beautiful time with me. She'd been terribly depressed—and I'd helped her over it. She felt this magazine, even though I was far from these people, was an indictment of me. She had to really go in the bathroom and get control of herself to keep from yelling out, God damn you! How dare you! And she said she felt no identity with this magazine, none, though she'd been to bed with me millions of times, and she remembered that I always used to say, when she was talking about things and she'd say, Do Lesbians do such and such a thing, and I used to say, What do you think *you* are? And she'd say, I'm not. And she said she knew she was right, and I know she was right now too. She wasn't. She was a woman who had a Lesbian experience.

The difference is this. It's a way of life. Don't you know when people are saying, Get the faggots and Down with Lesbianism, they're not picking on what people are doing in bed! They aren't at all. They're picking on *the way of life.*

They're picking on faggots who swish around, they're picking on me who wears my pants down the street and looks at women, they're picking on a way of life. Nobody would even care or know what goes on in bed.

I have orgasms with men. I'm built high. That's a great advantage. If your clitoris is high, as a man rides you, you come faster. And it isn't purely mechanical because I like men. I usually like them to leave immediately. I don't like them there the next day. I mean, men are very noisy, they turn the radio on, they snort and gargle, and everything, and they have these big shoes and they clomp around—they make so much noise. And they want to get up early on Sundays, and they want to get eggs scrambling. I've probably had more men than women. But I've remembered them less.

My mother hates cats. She asked me, Why are Lesbians always in love with cats? Maybe you could answer that? And I said, I don't know, Mother, you'd have to ask a Lesbian. Knowing full well she was asking one. She doesn't bug me, I bug her. Purposely sometimes. Once, when my mother was here, I confronted her openly with my homosexuality, because I told her—very meanly told her. I was mad at her. Then she wrote me a letter saying she's been on tranquilizers ever since that news, and she thought my moving to New Mexico was a mistake and that New Mexico was making me queer. And so I wrote back and said on the contrary, I was making New Mexico queer. So she sent that letter to my father, who ignored it—he ignores everything along those lines. He feels homosexuality is like communism—once it's banned, I'll come out of it.

The only thing my father ever said to me about it—
we were drinking heavily, many years ago, after my
mother had written the letter and I was up there
with a girl, and he took a great liking to her and spent
a good percent of the time trying to make out with her—
when she was in the bathroom once, he said, You know,
I've always been deaf, and I've always felt that anybody
that was worth anything had an incapacity, and they
had to rise above it. Look around you, there's Roosevelt,
and he rattled off a list of names and then he said, You
know, Dorothy, for years, I wondered about your success, and why you had made it. . . .

**VANESSA and JOHN, ANTHONY and SALLY.
These young lovers, whose ages range from twenty
to twenty-four, have set up housekeeping together
while trying to finish their degrees. They are deep
into the struggle of moving close to one another
while each tries to find a personal identity.
Consequently there are many strains on their
relationships, and they feel uncertain about the
future. Their day-to-day lives are further
complicated by worrying about their parents and
their desire to be good children to their parents
as well as good lovers to each other.**

VANESSA: I believe in marriage fully, simply from the
    aspect of children. I love children and want to have
    lots of them, but I don't think people should rush
    into marriage. You have to provide a good environ-
    ment for the children.
JOHN: I believe in the institution of marriage, but I
    believe living together before is really a tremendous

idea. I've never had any problem about women, but there is some fear of "the other." It all depends on if you get a submissive chick. Vanessa is becoming more submissive. She's mellowing.

VANESSA: Like the way I am with John is, I go as far as I can, I push him as far as I can, but as soon as he barks back I get scared. I want him to control me.

SALLY: Anthony does control me. I get pleasure out of taking care of him—cooking breakfast and so on. I might complain about it, but I like him to say that I've *got* to do it.

VANESSA: It's like a tango. You take turns being boss.

JOHN: And that makes it equal. You know at first you say, Oh, WOW! we're living together, we're doing our things. Then after the novelty wears off, the things about real marriage start to hit home. Like getting up in the morning, and she goes in the bathroom and does her thing, and smears makeup all over the sink, and you want to go in and shave. And you're tense, and you're uptight because the eggs don't come out right. When we first started together, she had this boyfriend that she was seeing every Saturday night, because that was his only free night. So comes the Saturday night and she says she has to go out. And I said, Ohhhhh? This has been going on till just a couple of weeks ago. The first few Saturdays I sat home, until I met this other chick one day, so I told Vanessa she couldn't stay over all night because I might want to sleep with this new girl. Well, we had a big scene.

VANESSA: And I stopped going out with that other boy.

JOHN: I don't know how long we are gonna last, but for now we're having a great experience; if we blow up and end it, nobody's gonna be really crushed. It's not like a divorce.

ANTHONY: It's different in our case, we've been living together a lot longer than you two.

SALLY: I couldn't say what John says, about it's a good experience and all that if you break up. I'm really jealous, very, very jealous—extremely possessive. That's kind of bad because I'll get jealous of just any little tiny thing that Anthony does. I'm extremely dependent on him, because my parents aren't around. I have no brothers or sisters—so the only person I really have is Anthony. If we ever broke up I'd just go right through the ceiling, I would freak out!

ANTHONY: She keeps hassling me about a commitment for settling this whole thing with something like marriage. But I'm really afraid, because I don't know what I'm going to be doing, or how long I'm going to be living—so I don't want to commit myself. There's something about that that really freaks me. I never say anything to her that will sound permanent.

VANESSA: I'm super close with my parents. But my mother's got this colossal temper, like mine. When we were little she'd blow up to the point where I actually thought she was going to leave us, so I've been insecure and kept off balance ever since. It didn't seem to bother my brothers and sister though. But my dad I like. We can communicate without talking.

JOHN: They complement each other.

VANESSA: But I have a shorter temper than my dad. I blow up, but it only lasts two minutes.

JOHN: That's not true.

VANESSA (laughing): It is true.

JOHN: You brood. You're a brooder.

VANESSA: I'm not. (Sighs)

JOHN: It's been my experience from observing you that when something's bothering you you're close-mouthed. . . .

VANESSA: Yeah, I won't talk about it.

JOHN: And when you do, it's a very low-toned kind of I-just-better-watch-my-step condescension.

VANESSA: Yeah?

JOHN: That's the only thing that hassles me about you, is your moods.

VANESSA: I know, I'm really moody, really moody.

SALLY: Anthony just completely freaks out when he blows up.

ANTHONY: See, I have a thing inside of my head, inside of me, that keeps tightening up. Some days it comes on me more often. I'm really excited and tense inside, and she'll drop a pencil and I'll start coiling up. And then all of a sudden for no reason I start coming apart and I lose all touch with reality and everything blacks out. I go into a fury, and WOW, it's FANTASTIC—I just FLY.

SALLY: He's come this close to hitting me or knocking me dead.

ANTHONY: But I'd always stop. It's a carry-over from when I used to be in a gang, when I'd get in a fight, I'd black out for like a couple of minutes at a time and just go completely crazy on someone and practically kill them—sort of like an animal.

SALLY: It still does frighten me a great deal, but I figure it's something inside his head, so I try my best to help him. So usually when he does it, I go over there and put my arms around him. I have to always be the one to call him back. If we have a fight, I have to go running after him. He walks out, I have to do the track thing and find out where he is, stuff like that. Another thing, when he starts tightening up like that, it irritates me. . . . So he gets all uptight and I do too. It's like I start pushing him, maybe it's sadistic, maybe it's what I want— so he explodes, and then I go after him, and so that's the end, and then we're fine. Our arguments and fights are over really fast. We make up, really, a lot. That's the major part of what we do is make up.

JOHN: It takes a while when you're living together. It's taken me about a month to find out all of the little things that I do that irk Vanessa and vice versa. We've been sleeping together about a year. . . .

VANESSA: And living together about two months.

JOHN: I must confess that I try to correct my faults, but if I think she's beginning to get the upper hand, I know just what to do to get back at her.

ANTHONY: When you really want to destroy somebody, you pick up all the little things you know will burn someone, and you just SCREW it right in there. And I do that sometimes. Like I'll sit down at the table sometimes and Sally will be hassling me in the morning, and if she hassles me too much, I go, ARGHHHHHH these eggs are ROTTEN. And, man, you look, oh, you look, oh, you look really BAD. I really know how to get to her, really.

SALLY: He won't come to the table on time, and when I put down the food, I want him to eat it right away. Every time at dinner time, right when I have it ready, he has to make a phone call.

VANESSA: John has to get all his clothes on before he comes to breakfast.

SALLY: Anthony does that too, he does that too. And he won't get up and he won't get up. I have to take the covers off him and then he gets mad.

ANTHONY: Tell about the time we were stoned and you started floating away. Oh, wow!

SALLY: Okay, there was this one time we were smoking and it was Brazilian super grass, something fantastic. And I started listening to the music—I've never had this experience before—I could see myself in this kind of little cubicle, floating through space. It was really bad. And I thought, Listen, I'm floating away just forever and ever. If I don't hold onto something like Anthony, I'll be lost, I'll be dead, I'll be gone forever. So I held on desperately to be near him. And I had to go to the bathroom and I made him go with me. And ever since then whenever we smoke or anything, I have to be near him. It's really a strange experience. I think it's part of depending on him a lot.

ANTHONY: Yeah.

VANESSA: You just have to jump into things. If you're gonna get married, do it. Even living together can't help you to decide to get married. Just say to yourself, okay, I'm gonna get married and do it! I'm not talking about me. I don't know if it's possible to live with someone the rest of your life. I haven't known that many men to decide. The decision of who to spend your life with is ungodly, it's immense. How can you make such a decision at the age of twenty-one?

JOHN: I think basically the same thing, except that—I

kind of disagree with you, Vanessa. I think that you
can find out in living together . . . .

VANESSA: But you can't be sure.

JOHN: No, you can't be sure, but that's always a risk.
It's a very tremendous thing to do, because you learn
immensely about little things about people. Little
things that really make up a person you know.

VANESSA: It's the little things that tell you whether or
not you can live with that person.

JOHN: One very important point is that you realize the
complexity of what you're dealing with, you know.
You realize that this isn't just two people sleeping
together and having a good time at night—this is
something that's really big, and that can be a very
very fantastic thing as the years go by. And I can
see how you can just get more and more and more
in love, y'know, as the years pass or at the same
time just go farther and farther apart. That's why
that decision is so important. That's why I think
it's a fabulous idea to live together and to try to
create an environment which is as much like the
institution of marriage as possible, without actually
doing it. It certainly can't be based on sex! (A gentle
laugh) You find that out after a week. There's been
a lot of times when we've climbed into bed and not
even touched, just, you know, rolled over and gone
to sleep. *And* then a lot of other times when we
couldn't stay away from each other. So you know,
you find out it's not a constant thing that you can
depend on, you know. It's gotta be something else
—and it's trust, that's what it is.

VANESSA: It's like I was going through this big hassle, and
I had this vast infection, and he couldn't come near

me, and it went on for over a week, and we couldn't
do anything. But I slept with him, and we were just
like together.

ANTHONY: If you're gonna live together—it's a gas, but
there isn't any set formula. You just have to experiment. I'm not ready for marriage, I'm really young,
y'know, I have a lot to learn about living and life
and people and things. Marriage is such a big thing,
choosing someone you're gonna be with for the rest
of your life! I'm not set to make it—not anywhere
in the foreseeable future. (Glance at Sally) Did
you hear that?

SALLY: I think that you should experiment before you
get married to see if you could make it. Like I
always used to believe in boarding school that you
could live with love, you don't have to have sex.
Well, Anthony was the first one, still the only one,
that I've ever been to bed with. The way I see it,
it's all a part of a thing called love. The way I see it
now, I don't think I could make it with anyone else.
It might all change later on, but I don't think so.
Did you hear that, Anthony?

ANTHONY: Yes.

**ANN McCRAY, twenty-six. A former nun, she now
works as a second-grade schoolteacher. She races
home each day to work on her films. She's crazy
about film-making and has applied to graduate
school to learn more about the art.**

The five of us eat together and give each other emotional support. It'll be a year this August for me here.

We have a community now of four women and a man.

I think this communal thing has evolved because of the isolations we've experienced in our families. Families don't understand your emotional needs. They feed you, and they put clothes on your back, but if you have a problem, like with a man, or some other emotional hangup, they can't relate to it. They find it very difficult to think that you're disturbed in any way.

When I came out of the convent, I needed lots and lots of affection, but I didn't get enough, I wanted it at twenty-three, and twenty-four, and twenty-six. All the time I was in the convent (five years) I wanted to give myself to other people for a certain cause, and I chose the order because of the spirit of the order. Spirit means the joyous caring for other people and being really human to them. I was seventeen when I went in. I made my commitment in the seventh grade.

I guess that's not a really big thing, because I didn't believe I could get married. I didn't have any boyfriends. I don't know why—maybe it was my personality or I wasn't pretty enough—I know I wasn't whole. Boys were always like buddies, I could work with them, got along well with them, but I didn't flirt with them. I wanted it, but I didn't know how to do it or how to give it.

Mother was glad when I tried to be a nun, but she knew all the time that I could never make it. She told me when I came out. She didn't say anything before, because I'm too damn headstrong. I would have run away. I would have gone in anyway, I wouldn't have believed her.

I was in love with Jesus. I really dig what his philosophy is and what he wants to do for people. Where it's at is this loving Christian type of brotherhood. When you go in you make a commitment to God, and to the community, and to yourself that you're going to live out the vows of poverty, chastity, and obedience to the best of your ability. Our order received no wedding rings at the time of going in, but other orders have them. Now that our order is out of the habit, the nuns are buying rings as a protective measure, so men won't try to seduce them. They go in the church now and the boys whistle at them.

When I was in, I had the habit on, I had no trouble with men because they respected the habit. I didn't like it that they treated me that way. Like you'd get a flat tire on the highway, suddenly there's four cars there. Just because of the damn habit. You stand in line for a movie, and someone says, Oh, here, come on—and you get in free. I didn't like being a privileged person.

You know, I was *told* to leave the order. They didn't let me make my own decision. I think if I could have made my own decision, I would have left on my own. They said I had tremendous spirit. You're really with it, they said, but you just don't have the vocation. That was the phrase they used—You just don't have the vocation.

They drove me crazy trying to make me walk like a nun. Nuns have certain images you have to abide by. You have to speak a certain way. You couldn't say, Yeah and Wow and Great. You couldn't go up to anybody and say, Hi! You'd have to say, Good afternoon.

When you'd get these weird vibes coming in—these sex feelings—you had to confess them. A friend of mine was cloistered; the nuns couldn't even talk to each other, so they used to pass love notes. The nuns were starting to fall in love with each other because they had no release.

I was six months in the postulance, and a year as a

novice, which means you have the white veil on, and you're actually living the life of a nun. It was fantastic at first—I really dug it. Honest to God, I don't regret it. It was the most fantastic spiritual experience I've ever had. I didn't have a hard time in the novitiate; most do. But I never had a hard time with myself being a nun, it was that I wasn't grooving with how they said I was supposed to be. I always used to wear my belts low, and you had to wear them up at the waist.

When you confess your sex vibes to the priest, he might tell you to open up a pillow and pick up all the feathers as a penance. But usually he tells you to pray, or smile at people and see how many people you can get to smile at you. If you get a groovy priest, then you get a groovy penance. But confession is fucked up anyway; I never go now. I'm too good. I don't have any bad things to confess and I never did.

Women are being allowed to read the epistle in church now. That's the latest from Rome. But women are never allowed on the altar except to clean it and put flowers up there, or change the candles. But everybody's leaving the priesthood, so maybe the women will get in there anyway.

I've been in love three times since I've been out, but I haven't slept with a man yet. I want to get married one of these days and have kids and bring them up the way I want to.

In the underground mass you're relating to people. You're with your friends, and you're breaking bread together. And you have them in your home whenever you can. We have about thirty who come once a week, or we meet in the park. There is dialogue, or dinner, or we read something from the Bible, or I'd show a movie and we'd talk about it. Sometimes an underground priest would lead, sometimes we'd all read the consecration together. With your words, you change the bread into His body, and the wine into His blood. Last summer two priests, two nuns, and a brother and I had an all-night mass in La Jolla. We all slept together, and before we went to bed, we had bread and wine, and anybody could make up their own words. We all cuddled up and cooed together. I love Jesus, I call Him Sam when I talk to Him.

MARSHALL and LORETTA MOBERG. This warm and loving couple are in their mid-thirties. They have given away their television and radio, and have given up reading the daily papers. There is very little furniture, only what's absolutely necessary to them. The walls are hung with some of Marshall's paintings. The children whom they've adopted have decorated any other available wall space. They are devoted to each other, their children, and friends with whom they correspond.

MARSHALL: Our marriage is pretty successful, I'd say. We lived together a couple of years before we did it legally. I'd never considered marrying anyone but Loretta.

LORETTA: Both of us had had sexual relations with other people. The first night we slept with each other, then we never parted again. I'd had some very serious involvements with men before I met Marshall. Some of these good people wanted to marry me, but it never worked out. I know that these relationships led me to appreciate Marshall more than if I'd met

him first. With Marshall, I didn't want to go home
after sex. I wanted to stay with him and eat and
talk and travel. My parents had had a good marriage
in Sweden, but my mother died when I was seventeen; she gave me a great deal of security, and I
had her when I needed her as an adolescent. There
was never any time for a mother/daughter problem,
and my father let me go to a university. I used to
write, but I'm much more interested in doing things,
and raising the children. I want to know more ways
of being alive with other people. I wrote a few
books, and I didn't get anything out of it but money
and good reviews. My life didn't change because of
writing them, as I'd hoped it would.

MARSHALL: This was sort of the thing that happened to
me too. I had a one-man show at about the same
time that two of her books came out, and we were
both enormous successes, but it didn't make any
genuine difference in our essential lives. Then we
became a husband and wife team in Chicago and
worked together, but we found it was difficult, and
had to watch out that it didn't become destructive.

LORETTA: It doesn't mean that we try not to disagree, but
we try to live very close. I was so upset last night,
for example, to think that Marshall would have to
go away for a few days to see about a job in another
city. We had some terrible scenes, and later ended
up both crying and we finally found out what it was
all about, and it was all about that neither one of us
wanted to be separated from the other. We are very
honest with each other, but it's sometimes hard to
know right away what's troubling us, but we usually
can get to it. Actually we've been separated so little
since we've been close together, and we've never

slept away from each other since we've had the children. And I think very often we do lose our tempers with each other because we are so close.

We can practically read each other's minds, but I think it's more that we're in touch with each other's thoughts and feelings. I know that I feel very incomplete, emotionally disturbed, even what people might call crazy when we are apart.

MARSHALL: Most people in marriage don't want to tell the other person what they're really thinking about. Like this friend of ours turned up here one day with a very pornographic book that he'd bought at the airport. He minimized it and put it down, but knowing him, I knew he'd read every word of it and been excited by it, but he'd never told his wife that he even bought that sort of book. This guy does this every time he goes off on a trip, but he doesn't even know anything about his wife. It might turn out that she's reading books like that while he's gone. Here they could have been doing this together. But any time they think they're doing something that doesn't fit conventional behavior, they become alienated from other people, including their own spouse.

LORETTA: Both of us came from parents who had all sorts of problems, but they were physically very close. They always slept together and talked about their love in front of us.

MARSHALL: My father always kissed my mother when he left the house and when he returned. But I have friends who never saw their parents kiss.

LORETTA: And Marshall and I may have fights three nights a week that sound terrible to other people, but we always make up right away—if we have a problem we have to attack it at once and work it out. We don't tolerate anything coming between us.

MARSHALL: Sometimes the children don't understand our fights, they try to soothe us. They come and say, It's gonna be all right. They copy us, of course. On my father's side of the family nobody talks. They're all absolutely silent about emotional things. I still have some of this problem. What our fights are about is that Loretta is usually trying to get me to admit something because I'm acting like a maniac, pacing up and down and breathing like a werewolf, and I keep maintaining nothing's wrong. I like to go around in the nude; even as a boy I was always in ripped clothing and shirts with no backs in them, and I realized that my father always slept nude, and sometimes he'd come down in the middle of the night and make himself a sandwich and he'd be wearing no clothes, while I'd be having a party with my friends. To this day my mother will never admit that my father appeared anywhere in our house in the nude. We have terrific problems with my mother. I had to finally refuse to see my parents because of it. Not that I mean I'd never see them, but for the first two years of our marriage, it just wasn't possible.

Regardless of how well Loretta says she got on with her own mother, I know she's transferred some of her problems with her mother onto my mother.

LORETTA: She tried to make another child of me. I didn't want that, I'd been trying to get away from home so that I *could* become an adult.

MARSHALL: And of course my mother had the usual hangup that men are better than women, and that's the big problem today. It's a worldwide problem.

LORETTA: I was brought up in Sweden and my mother

was the same way. Of course her own father was very tyrannical and thought that girls were no good, so my mother's attitude toward all us girls was very grotesque. When she finally had a son, she almost went wild. She'd suffered so much because of what she thought was the difference between men and women but she just couldn't change. She did make sure that we girls went to the university and were able to support ourselves. I think a lot of it went back to the fact that my mother thought that if she had a male child her father would then love her.

MARSHALL: Loretta and I still have to fight these things out together. We, too, still represent to each other these things we've been taught by our parents. I was brought up by my mother as a favored son, with special privileges, and Loretta, with her brother brought up the same way, is still very ready for that trouble. So you can see our arguments are right there, they're all set up before we even start. We don't want to be this way, but we're still suffering from those things of two generations ago. I mean that's as far back as we personally know. We're very seriously trying to stop this stuff because it only makes us unhappy.

LORETTA: It's hard, it's a lot of work and it's exhausting.

MARSHALL: We just thought of this yesterday: there's something about our arguments that isn't like us.

LORETTA: It's schizophrenic. It's a fight of two other people where our essential personalities are not truly involved.

MARSHALL: Like I say, I'm going to leave and never come back, but that isn't true. Some of these problems aren't really our own.

LORETTA: We don't want our kids to suffer from the hangovers.

MARSHALL: This is not something we've been aware of for a long time, it's twelve years of working it out.

LORETTA: One thing is that I didn't conceive any children, and we had time to work out our difficulties together, before we adopted these babies.

MARSHALL: We see so many people that deserve to live together for the rest of their lives. They're perfectly each other's equals, but they separate, they don't work these things out. And it's usually something that they can't talk about with each other. The more we work things out and the more I see how things of the past can mar the present, the more I think if you were free of hangups, you could almost marry anybody and be perfectly happy. But the only way I see my friends marry, it looks like they're out to find the most complicated relationship possible that will fit in with the hangovers of their past and their parents' pasts. Take computer dating: people are trying to meet someone who will meet all these complex requirements, someone who won't disturb the configurations. They go through fantastic machinations to find what they think they need.

LORETTA: But I do think people have to have something to hold them together. We're very intense people and very close.

MARSHALL: But we also come from two different continents. Right away it makes for a big difference in the way we've been brought up and our expectations and way of thinking.

LORETTA: But I don't think in, or even speak, Swedish any more.

MARSHALL: One of the reasons we were able to adopt children, and interracially mixed children at that, is because we got rid of so many old patterns.

LORETTA: We always wanted children from the first times we slept together. We never used contraceptives. Whereas with people I slept with earlier in my life, I was always careful about it. Even the first night with Marshall, I didn't.

MARSHALL: Like the first night I said something about, It's all right? and she said, Yes, and that's all we ever said about it again.

LORETTA: We'd known each other for about six weeks. I had an apartment of my own. He'd come and visit me, and we'd talk all night long and he'd go home and then come back the next day.

MARSHALL: We got tired eventually and went to bed. Actually by then I'd told her everything I had to say, we knew each other as best we could at that point . . . so . . . (Much laughter)

LORETTA: We didn't really know each other, but it seemed like we did. The reason we waited so long to adopt children was not anything to do with finances, but with wanting to have our own, plus to grow up. It was really after Marshall had this final fight with his mother and gave up smoking that we decided to adopt a child.

MARSHALL: I think people are afraid of not continuing with their blood line. The fear of not producing a blood descendant for their parents keeps many people from adopting children.

LORETTA: In my family all my sisters and brothers are having children. And actually my father's bored with it all, so it isn't so hard on me. But with

Marshall being an only child, and his mother being
an only child, I think there was a very strong feeling there that he should produce a blood child. I
don't think Marshall really felt like perpetuating . . .

MARSHALL: I can think of a lot of things I wouldn't want
to perpetuate.

LORETTA: She brought Marshall up very conscious of his
background.

MARSHALL: Her father used to take her on his knee and
tell her, You are bone of my bone, and flesh of my
flesh. Now he had a big problem in that his father
was killed in the Civil War before he ever saw
him, and this is another hangover from another side
of that family. There has always been a certain
morbidity and fear of the destruction of that side
of our family simply from that. But eventually we
realized that this had nothing to do with *our* lives.
Once the children are here, they're children, and it
sort of doesn't matter where they come from.

LORETTA: After all, they're interracial. . . .

MARSHALL: And they need parents. . . .

LORETTA: And we need children. . . . It's so easy to get
them. They have a lot of them.

MARSHALL: As long as you'll take children not from the
same race as you are, there's no trouble at all. Once
you decide that you want children because you
want to make your own life happy and complete,
and perhaps help children and not please your parents, then *any* children become possible.

LORETTA: And now, we must think of the children, too.
My doctor told me he could probably make it possible for me to have a natural child, but I would
rather adopt another one, because it would make

it better for the children we already have to do this. The child would be more like them than like us, and it would be better for their growing up.

MARSHALL: The doctor undoubtedly feels that we have not given up the idea of perpetuating our tribe.

LORETTA: It satisfies me so much to see how more and more the children get along together. We got our boy last June, and I sort of regard the children as my job. I've never been so happy in a job before, and I've worked. Our boy was so tense when we got him, but he's more relaxed and he gets around and becomes more and more aggressive. Unless you get them directly from the hospital, it takes them so long to get over that frown, that little frown that's right there in the middle of the forehead. Our little girl, it took her until Christmas before she'd let anybody pick her up, but now she jumps right in your lap. But we've worked very closely with them, we have never had any baby-sitters. Our little boy was very disturbed at being brought here, he just wouldn't sleep for months. The way we got him to sleep was to constantly hold him and to always be nice to him, to sort of believe in the change, and it did happen. It was slow. He's thirteen months now. He was happy in the daytime, but at night it was hard on him. We had to give him his bottle all night long. But it's been important that we adopted them at a time when we had a lot of love for each other and time to devote to them. We've also made a point with them that they are not going to be brought up by me, but by *both* of us. We both hold them a lot, and Marshall changes them as much as I, and I'm not the only one to get shit under my fingernails.

**BUZZ SCHOENHOLTZ, a thirty-year-old executive
in the garment industry, is in love and on the verge
of marriage. He believes his relationships with
women have helped him to grow up. He adores
New York City and wouldn't live anywhere else.
The city is his neighborhood. He is never frightened
and goes out to the theater almost every other night.**

Marriage is just a matter of formalizing a relationship.
It's all in people's minds. It's the relationship of two
people or more. I've got a typical J.M. [Jewish Mother],
you know, but she doesn't pressure me, she keeps talking but I've ignored her for all these years. There really
isn't that much pressure, it's unimportant. It isn't important that I be married. Some firms do worry if you're
married—more stable and all that.

People get married—like you've heard this a million
and a half times—the man gets married for a steady
piece and the woman gets married for security. It
shouldn't work that way, but that's what it is.

It took me a good number of years to regurgitate the
crap I'd been fed about success. What's so great about
being the greatest lover or the greatest businessman?
I've learned you're not gonna be good the first time in
bed because you've got to know somebody. It's the easiest thing in the world to strip down in the nude and
hop into bed—it's easy. But when you're doing something like that you're really performing. Like the first
time, it's not gonna be the greatest thing in the world.
It could be a few months or even years before you
achieve that physical union.

I don't think the "dating bars" are the best place
to meet lasting companions. Like I met my woman on

a Fire Island ferry. We talked, she got in touch with me
about two weeks later, and we started seeing one another. She's a teacher and lives out on the island. I've
stayed over with her, but it's so awkward because she
rents a room in a house with this family. Whenever I
went out there we were in different rooms, so very early
in the a.m. she'd have to get up and go back to her own
room.

My woman says she's gone through a great deal of
change since she's known me. Apparently the guys she's
gone out with have always used her. It was heartbreak-
ing that people didn't realize what a wonderful person
she was, what a wonderful human being. I would say
that a lot of men use women this way.

I think most women keep up the double standard
as much as men. They enter into a physical relationship
where the ultimate must be marriage and if it isn't they
feel terrible. They feel like a whore. I think women feel
that getting married is like getting a job. Society is hard
on women this way—like if a woman isn't married,
there's something wrong with her, but if a guy isn't married, they think he's a swinging bachelor. Sixty girls
a night and they envy you. But the important thing is
to find another person. You can love more than one
person, but human beings only have so much capacity
—to pour everything into one person and receive back
from that person. What I want now is a constant rapport.

If you had too many people, you'd be too diffuse.
Between you and I, I think my woman and I will get
married soon. We have this tremendous rapport with
each other. Women have had a tremendous effect on my
life—I look back on myself when I was younger and
Euyeckkk!!!! Women have helped me mature. Indirectly.
Just being with them and listening a bit.

I went with an older woman for a good number of years, and at the outset of the relationship I told her it wasn't going to be permanent, it could be broken at any time. I didn't want to kid her along. I encouraged her to go out and see other people. It was a good relationship, very comfortable, kind of strained at times, but when it got to be too strained, I wanted to forget it. It got to be too self-defeating—seeing her mainly for sex. It was constant; like every week. But I didn't exploit her for sex. I didn't like just go over there and have dinner and go to bed. It was a good growth relationship. But she was uptight. Like we couldn't kiss in public 'cause she was ashamed of going with a younger guy. What would people think! She had a great many problems. I broke off once and then I went back. I never kidded her. And she told me she was going out with other people. I always encouraged her to do that.

I enjoy sex. It's like a good meal, a good glass of liqueur, a good flick. Essentially what does it amount to? Only a few minutes—a few seconds—THE climax. It isn't the most important thing. It's good to have in any kind of sustained relationship, but I don't feel I own anyone. My woman can do whatever she wants. I honestly don't think I would be hurt if she slept with anyone else, because I know she loves me. It depends on the reasons you go with someone. If you go with them to wrack up a score, you're in trouble. But the whole thing is, we love each other!

I think my mother married my father for money. It was during the Depression. My father was a very wealthy man, he was working for the post office!

They constantly argue and fight. My mother still constantly spends money. I speak to my mother every day on the phone and she loves my girl. But all my family knows is going to Bingo and gossip. They don't involve themselves with anything.

The average individual gives more time to his job than anything else. Really, a job is a marriage. Just go on the basis of time—minimum of eight hours a day. For executives, twelve, fourteen hours. This is where the marriage is. The family is more or less like window dressing. Take the people who live in suburbia, they get up at the crack of dawn, travel a couple of hours to the job, spend eight hours, get back on the train, get home, eat, sleep. The kids don't even know their fathers.

Where my girl works, she tells me these people have these beautiful homes in suburbia, but they're empty. It's really sad—it was brought home so graphically. I had some imitation fur, left over from some coats we were making. So I gave it to the kids where my girl teaches. Well, these kids just loved it. They've never had rugs on their floors. They don't know what a rug is. All they have is a house . . . they hardly have any furniture, bed, a chair, a table. They don't make enough money to do anything but pay off the mortgage. The kids went fantastic over the rugs. I got a whole raft of thank-you notes. And these kids are second-graders. What do these kids have?—A television and a floor. No rugs.

MARTINE SIMS is twenty-four, black, and works as a counselor to teen-agers in Harlem. She has three advanced degrees and likes to sing up a storm at parties. Her father is a brain surgeon, and her mother works with civic groups in a large Mid-American city.

Martine has just racked up her new car. She laughs as she describes the accident and then tells an epic about all the automobiles she's owned that have been stolen and/or demolished. School seems so easy for her she's thinking of knocking off her Ph.D. while holding down two jobs.

My mother was right, I'm an alkie, I don't care. It's one of the better things, I really dig it. I like to drink better than anything else that there is to do. Look, I know I can, if I want to, I can set the bottle down. I can pick that bottle right back up. (She gestures with her beer.) I don't look it, but I'm a physical wreck. My spine is welded together, I have an ulcer, I'm anemic, I drink like a fish, I smoke like a . . . I had asthma as a child, but I decided to get rid of it, so I got rid of it.

My true love, the most fantastic man I've ever met— he died. That's the reason we're not together. I met him when my mother was going through menopause. We couldn't get along, so I moved to the dorms. And I met him. He was so rich, thrown out of six schools. His father owned half of U.S. Steel.

I met him at this party. He made some crack about my boobs, so I took a pitcher of grape juice and poured it all over his white shirt and his white duck pants. He picked me up and threw me in the bathtub. Then we lived together for three or four months. It took me a while to get to like lovemaking because I'd been raped when I was seventeen. I don't know why somebody wants to attack and rape me. But it was fall and I love to walk in fall. Some men were unloading a truck. And one guy said, Oh, aren't you cute, and I said, Fuck you. They jumped me. There were three of them, but only one raped me, thank God. It blew my mind, dig it, my head started getting completely fucked up. I cried a lot, I screamed a lot, but I could only scream for so long because he got his hand around my neck. They slugged me and I went out, then they left me. I didn't tell the police.

My mother knows that I was attacked and raped but she does not know the extent to which it fucked up my head. I'm very secretive with my parents. I don't want to hurt my mother so I don't tell them anything. I still don't until I'm far enough away from it so that I can be totally intellectual and totally unemotional about it.

I went back to the dorm. One of my roommates' father was in the Kennedy Administration and he was in town. The two of them virtually took care of me for about two days—I stayed drunk—and I sort of pulled myself together. I didn't pull myself together, I functioned on an automaton type level for a while, then I made these great, great decisions like, Well, my life is really fucked up now, so I might as well fuck it up some more. Oh yeah, completely. You got to remember, despite my outbursts and things like that, I was a Catholic, very middle-class, very protected. I was really a little, little girl, so for someone to attack and rape me, I mean, I'm not good for anything. I'm horrible, I'm ugly, I'm sinful, I'm corrupted. I'm evil, pure and simple evil.

After the rape, I went out and slept with some guys. Yes, I did some not too nice things. The chick's father who took care of me for two days, I started an affair with him. It wasn't a matter of sex, it was guilt. It's a guilt thing. "I am so ugly and so horrible and so evil, somebody punish me." People I really care about who were only trying to help me, I would lash out at them. Like my roommate—picking her father to have an affair with. It was pretty raunchy. She didn't know then, but eventually in my madness I told her.

My honey and I broke up because he was leaving to go to spend his remaining months in Germany and Switzerland, with his family. See, he died of leukemia. I knew he was sick. I found out the January before we broke up. I had been surrounded by so many good loving people in my life that there's no way . . . people have been too good for me in order for me . . . I'm not bitter, I've been surrounded by too much warmth and too much love.

In January when I found out, it was one of these things where I said, Look, we're going to get married. Because I really wanted to have his child. I loved him. We hadn't known he was ill. He'd been tired and very depressed and very—he was having pains, "I'm getting old" or something like that. He was twenty-seven. We did this great thing. He said, Okay, you want to marry, but we're going to take a trip first. So we went to Chicago for a weekend and while we were in Chicago, we went to a cancer ward at the University of Chicago's hospital and for a solid day he forced me to be there, to be happy, to talk to people, to be jovial with people— you know, all the things that I do well. He forced me for a solid day to be surrounded by death in very unpleasant ways. He was accepting the idea of death. It might be just ego, but the times that it hurt him the most were the times we were together, because we had, without a doubt, the most magnificent love going. You would see us, if he were here right now, if this room were filled with seven million people, and I would be over in one corner talking with somebody and he'd be over in another corner talking with somebody, you would still know. People have remarked about this. You could feel the bond between us, you could feel it, you knew it. You know, I do things at parties like I get zonked and I drape myself over somebody and everything, and do things that could possibly make somebody jealous, and he'd smile and say, C'mere, will ya. Which is the other magnificent thing about him. First man who I have ever met in my entire life who would say, Shut up, and I'd get mad and huff and puff and rage and rant around and —Shut up. Would you just shut up?—you know, but gentle, incredibly gentle. He'd know when to say Shut up and when to let me go, the first man. I have a very hard time crying, I can't cry, I almost never cry. First man, first person I've ever met who would intuitively know when I needed to cry and in many different ways get me to the point where I would just let it all out.

I was going through this hassle with my mother that would really be tearing me up and I would be being tough: Oh, fuck her. Who needs her? What the shit— you know. And he'd come over, put his head on my lap, or talk to me, take me out for drinks. He was just marvelous—which is a hangup for me now. He forced me to break up with him to protect me and to protect himself, which is the only way it could have ended.

ROSSANO DANASI, thirty, an editor, met and married his wife in his native Italy. They have two young girls. He loves his children very much, but he is beginning to have trouble with his wife. He thrives on emotion, and she has withdrawn from him. This makes him feel that all the tension, the

color has gone out of his life. So now they have an "arrangement." He goes out looking for what he feels is missing at home.

Some people do break up, but no matter what their status, community, or wealth, they are always in trouble with themselves and their neighbors because of how people feel. No one wants to go to school and be called "bastard." And that's what happens if your parents are divorced.

It's very unusual for young people to live together in Italy like they do here. Here a girl of eighteen or nineteen can prove to her family that she can support herself. She can rent and maintain her own apartment. In Italy this is inconceivable. One of the problems is that the young people in Italy tend to get married as soon as possible to disentangle themselves from family surveillance. Even a man of twenty-five at home tends to live with his family. He lives and eats with his family, but he has, of course, a one-room screwing pad. We call it a stock yard, where we kill the victim, you know. There is a saying that all girls in Italy go to bed at ten because they have to be home by midnight.

My parents don't seem to worry too much about me being here, I guess they're rather unorthodox. I ran away from home when I was seventeen because I was in love with a Dutch airline stewardess, but I had to come back home because she flew somewhere else. My parents are embarrassed about me with other people, but they don't worry me about their thoughts. It's all a matter of trust. My parents trust both my sister and I, but this is contrary to most parents in Italy, they just don't trust their children.

In spite of all this restriction it's basically easy to go to bed with a girl as long as you have a screwing pad or a car. Usually Italian girls screw in cars.

My wife is American. I came here because I was fed up with Italy. I couldn't work there or be myself there. I knew I could work anywhere, so it was easy for us to come here. I've always been in publishing so I got a job after I'd been here two weeks. I have two girls. One is very beautiful and very bright. One is not so beautiful but she's very tender.

Our marriage is going along—I don't want to use the word "limbo"—but I think we've reached a kind of balance. You see, I used to be very violent, impulsive, but things that used to bother me a lot don't bother me so much any more. I'm just as nervous and neurotic, but not so violent. My wife helped to calm me. She used to be strong and energetic. She used to respond to my violence. In other words, I need tension, I need constant tension or I don't function well. I can't just live with a woman and make love and that's it. I need to fight, I don't mean fight for the hell of it. I need competition, I need tension—tension in the positive way. It's a way of intense communication. After a while, though, my wife decided to give up responding to me—she said it was self-defense because I was so violent and so intense. I felt all right as long as she was responding to me, but after a while—after a couple of years—she decided to withdraw and not to respond to my way of being and that of course resulted in a number of crises. But we've managed to stay together somehow. We've been married eight years. A lot of people who got married around the same time we did are either separated or divorced, but to last even five years any more is relatively amazing.

I could divorce very easily—we're in America and

it's very easy, but I think it's too easy a way out. When you have dedicated so many years of your life to another person, · you've developed something that's worth exploring. It's probably not even marriage any more. As far as marriage is concerned, I think it's over for us. We're not married in the usual sense, we really manage to live two separate lives.

I'm absolutely free to go and do and think and spend. I have total freedom. I have other affairs for one simple reason, because I need the tension. Frankly, we haven't discussed her freedom. She has the will to freedom, but she doesn't have the time because of her children. She's also gone back to school to study for her master's degree, because she eventually wants to teach.

In terms of orthodox marriage, ours is a failure, it doesn't exist. It's not a marriage any more. Her parents are horrified by my behavior and they disapprove of her response. They're very intelligent people, they realize we don't have an orthodox relationship. But somehow, we are four people who live together, who manage to communicate at all levels, so I don't see why I should impose traditional cliches onto my daughters. I don't have any program about how I'm going to raise them, but I don't act like a father. I spend time with them when I feel like it. I'm very passionate, very tender. We're very close to each other. We're a family. We have terrible fights, my daughters and I. They're very articulate. I can talk to them. They talk better than I do as a matter of fact. They even have better logic than I; of course their English is better. Their dialectic power is better, I can't cope with them sometimes. They're five and six. It's very funny, when I lose control of myself, they try to make me reason. They say, Calm down, that's how life is, and so on. The bright and beautiful one, she's learning to write now. And she has a very hysterical time with the work. She'd been told by the teacher to write about very simple things. "I love my mother because she buys me candy," and so on. But instead she wanted to write about what's going on with adults. She ended up screaming on the floor because she didn't know how to write it. She was yelling, I want to write it, but I don't know how to write it. I tried to calm her by telling her to write it by what she knows, what she's seen, what she's capable of imagining about adults, but all the rest—forget it. Then she was all right.

For the last five years our marriage has been nothing but habit. All the tension has gone out of it, and it makes me feel apathetic toward my work. I feel sterile. My wife withdrew first, and then I withdrew. She comes from a wealthy, healthy family. Went to good schools. She's a real woman, but very virginal in a sense. She likes songs and things that teen-agers like, not because she's stupid, but because she's young at heart.

I never lie to my wife, I hate to lie. I come in in the morning, and she says, What time did you get in, and I say, Six-thirty A.M. She says, Oh. She's a bit sad, but she shows nothing else. I wish she'd fight with me. I wish she'd yell at me. If she behaved with the total freedom that I do, I don't know how I'd react. Do I have the right to beat her up if she's unfaithful? I don't know. We're really best friends, we still sleep together and eat together. It's a very particular kind of friendship.

I can't stand people. She's the only human being whom I can stand to have around me. The only one. I can't stand to be bugged or disturbed. She protects me from people who try to call me on the phone, the outside world.

But our marriage is really a habit. I think habit is

more fundamental to the human being than sex. It's a monstrous thing, you get trapped. It's not only difficult to break this habit, it's impossible. We have this private language between us, it's inevitable when you have a relationship with someone for a number of years. Now this language is mostly silent, but it's your private channel. It's a vehicle between you to try to get to reality. But why break up with her? I'm in this habit, I can't get out of it—chances are if I got a new woman, I'd turn her into the same woman I have now.

I must say that I get very excited with men, and that's the trouble. Also with particular women, with whom I won't have a deep sexual relation, women who won't give up to me so easily.

Now my kids, they think they live in a family, they don't know about our arrangement, but they don't acknowledge my authority. Their mother's word is law. I have a passionate relationship with them, we play and fight, but they *believe* my wife.

I think the institution of marriage has reached a critical point all over the world. Because of the different social position of the woman. She's a human being, she can vote, she exists! She can be independent because she can get a job. There is together with this a deep crisis of authority. The man is not the man any more. This is at all levels. Information is power. Once only the man knew certain things. Now everybody watches television and everybody knows the same things. The man can't lay down the law any more by saying what he knows.

ROSE STANDISH is a professional woman, married, with two children. She is nearing retirement age and lives in the Midwest. She has a strong sense of family and has tried to give her children firm roots. She is looking forward to spending her retirement years with her husband in Florence, Italy.

I couldn't judge for anybody else whether marriage is good as an institution, but it certainly is for us—for myself. We have friends all over the United States and Europe whom we've know for years. Most of these people are still married, a few widowed, a very, very few divorced—whether this speaks well for the Midwest, I don't know.

When my daughter and her husband were contemplating—contemplating! it was like trying to hold back the Red Sea—and nobody was going to be the one to hold back the Red Sea, I said to her, trying not to pontificate, You simply must *not* confuse love and marriage, and I hope you aren't. Because they are not the same thing.

It's because people think it's like it is in the ladies' magazines, and think they want that for themselves. But I think we in the Midwest are less prone to that. We're more realistic. We know because our mothers and our grandmothers have told us how it was to win the West.

My daughter did know her grandmother, who filed a claim in the West. A remarkable woman who knew what it was like to live there. It's a kind of shape that your life has almost before you start on it. "These are

my roots, this is my background." And I can improvise
on it as much as I like. I was the first person in my
family to finish college all the way. It was not usual at
the time to assume that all the girls would go to college,
but in my family it was. Just about all of my cousins—
my father had four brothers and four sisters—went to
college.

I have so much going for me in my marriage because
of the nature of my husband's work and the nature of
the man himself. He's one of your great all-time listeners.
And he listens to everybody with exactly the same attention and respect. Democracy—it's so much a part of
the way we live. People are equally interesting, they are
equally valuable, equally important. So you live with
this feeling that anything you say is going to be lis-
tened to.

We certainly have had our fights. When the children were small, we spent about thirty percent of our
time at each other's throats. I mean just spitting angry.
I don't have any of these theories about kiss and make
up before you go to sleep—I believe in getting the
hostility right out in the open. This was very hard for
my husband, because of his natural courtesy. He's often
said to our children, The one thing your mother's taught
me was not to save up anger, but to let it out. In the
early days of our marriage, things would happen at the
office, he'd come home and not talk. Well, this is hard
on me who is a nonstop talker, and my heart would
break if he wouldn't talk to me. Sometimes he'd stay
silent for two or three days, and I'd be frantic. He didn't
like to see me frantic, so we began to work it out.

Marriage is the hardest thing in the world, there's
no question of it. Even if you start out honestly believ-
ing that *it*, the relationship itself, is more important than

I am or than *you* are—and this, I think, is very rare indeed.

I've thought a lot about this thing of a permanent relationship, and if you can think of one single reason in the whole world not to do it—don't! I mean even a one-night stand. I think you do yourself, finally, a disservice. You must be able to say yes to everything about the other person. I've never known a marriage to succeed where the man set about changing the wife. Now the people who weigh things in the balance—I've heard lots of them, particularly somebody embarking on his second or third marriage—and it's almost always a man, curiously enough—Well, of course, she has this, and it's true she doesn't have that, she's awfully good in bed, and she can cook, but she was awfully rude to my aunt the other day, or she's selfish, she goes into a room and pouts. . . . If you're gonna play that game, *don't get married!*

I don't mean to suggest that people together don't get better—they do. It's possible to grow up together, especially if you remember what it is you're working at, particularly if you have children you're onto something that isn't just "love." This is a little house you're building —what it is to be *this* family. I think too many parents are afraid to impose this on their children, while the children really want it imposed upon them. They want to be told, This is what it is to be a Smith. *The Smiths*—! It gives them something to revolt against just for starters. You should teach courtesy as much at home as at school, and this is not to say that absolutely blinding arguments don't go on among us.

When the children want to get under our skins, which they can do brilliantly, they start to talk among themselves: Remember when Mother and Daddy had that really knock-down, drag-out fight, and we couldn't decide whether they were drunk or whether they were really going to get a divorce? And we used to just cry because we thought Mother was going to leave us and move to a hotel.

My husband amounts to almost perfection. Some of the women where he works say to me casually, If something would just happen to you! That's how much he's wanted. But I don't think it hurts anyone who's sixty years old to be told over and over that he's an exceedingly desirable man. That's a compliment to both of us.

As for fidelity in marriage, I don't think it even relates to the success of it. Now, I'm talking about the casual infidelity, not an affair that's going on forever. I've never known it to cause a divorce, but then I'm just talking about my fine, upstanding. Cadillac-driving, Midwestern friends. It can temporarily rock a marriage, from one end of the shore to the other, and we always get told these stories, because they think we're some sort of ideal couple who never have these problems. They come to us with much tears and lamentations and beating of the head, then we usually remind them of something they have to do tomorrow, give them a drink, tell them to cool it, you've built this thing called marriage, and you just can't take it and throw it out the window. It's not just the children involved, it means to a great many people two people together who represent a certain life-style, a quality of mind and heart that they've learned to rely on. The minute you've built a marriage a whole hunk of you belongs to the world and not to you any more.

JOSÉ RODRIQUEZ and BILL ROVIN, twenty-two and twenty, are friends. They've just dropped out of college together and are fixing up a new apartment with the money that Bill's father thinks he's spending for Bill's education. They decided that their college courses were childish, made no sense to them, and were not preparing them for the real world. They've bought a movie camera to learn their work by trial and error, also a color TV, and stay up all night studying movie technique on the late-late show. José came to the States from Cuba when he was twelve; Bill has spent his life in private schools.

BILL: One of my grandmothers was really beautiful. She was married to this man who was a button manu-facturer. He worked for his money, he really did. And they loved each other like you wouldn't believe. They lived together for fifty-five years before he died.

JOSÉ: So this wonderful woman is dying of cancer, only she doesn't know it. What really got me is that just the mention of her husband's name, and she starts crying. . . .

BILL (a trace of wonder): The tears, you wouldn't be-lieve. And she starts saying, Oh, that man, I loved him so.

JOSÉ: They traveled all over the world, they were always together. Now the other grandmother obviously married the man for money. I'm not knocking that because as long as her husband lived she made him comfortable.

BILL: We have to explain the situation, because she was my father's secretary *and* lover. She's really my *step*-grandmother. She's a year older than my father. My real grandmother died. So this woman was my father's lover while he was still married to my mother. So she married my grandfather because he had more money than my father, right? Well, this turned my father's head inside out because the rest of his life was nothing but a competition with my grandfather. My father wouldn't speak to her again. But this woman raised me, she really did, and I loved her. But she really was out for the money because she's fighting me now. She came from a very middle-class, very well-established family in Boston. A very well-knit family. She and her sisters have ganged up to fight me.

JOSÉ: Now I know how the Jews have survived all these years—they're so close.

BILL: She wrote out her will and gave everything that was given to me to her sisters . . . this was brought out in court. She was so sure she'd win. When I found this out, my hair stood on end. Not that I wanted it, I told her she could do anything she wanted with the money, but I just couldn't believe she could do something like this.

JOSÉ: It's all pretense, all a sham.

BILL: I love her, and she'd *professed* to love me . . . .

JOSÉ: But she'd never take the responsibility, remember? She thinks that every man is after her for her money now. And she won't accept love from anyone.

BILL: There's a guy after her now, and he loves her, he *apparently* loves her and wants to marry her, but she won't marry him because she thinks he wants her money.

JOSÉ: But she won't even go out with men, because she thinks they'll grab at her purse.

BILL: She was a gold-digger and she doesn't want anybody to be a gold-digger to her. She gets a new Lincoln Continental every year. My father is in such a condition from everything that's happened in the last twenty years that he can't think straight. He's gone totally into business. He won't let himself think about his family. My mother's in an institution.

JOSÉ: Yeah, he put *her* away.

BILL: He totally ignored her. He's given his whole life to the business. He hurt so many people to get where he is—it's really tragic. He's a bundle of nerves. He smokes three or four packs of cigarettes a day and pops Librium into his mouth like it's going out of style. The nicotine is the oral stage. He never got beyond the oral stage, really . . . . He has to have one cigarette in his mouth and one in his hand. He can't see anybody else but himself . . . . He frightens me to death. Maybe he really doesn't have it but it *seems* like he has a lot of power. He's got brains, he's smart. He's dominated my life for so long, and he's shorter than I am! He's so secure, he seems to know where he's going, and he's established himself as far as money goes.

JOSÉ: He's very authoritative. He screams!

BILL: Before I met José, I'd do exactly everything my father would say.

JOSÉ: And I told him, See what it's done to your head that he makes you do all these things. Do you have a knife at your throat? *My* father's a great guy. They're old-money type thing. He had this money so he didn't have to exert himself too much, but now he's working like a pig. He works in this little place, he could never work in a big company. They leave him alone and he works there polishing metals. He comes home and he's very tired. And I can't understand it, he's just not *bitter* about it. All of a sudden, his whole life has changed and he's just accepted it. My mother, on the other hand, is very embittered. I think my mother reached thirteen and stayed at that age. She was a very very beautiful woman when she was young.

BILL: She still is.

JOSÉ: So she got married and she never had to think. Everything was done for her. Just do your thing, be feminine . . . . She was *kept*!

BILL: This is what's happening in America because everyone's becoming dependent on their parents, more so than ever, because everybody's becoming passive and not thinking. The militants aren't thinking either, it's more a reaction. Like they got to do something but they're not quite sure what. They'd rather use physical force than mental force. They'd rather go out and wreck a store than sit down and write a manifesto.

JOSÉ: It's all just a reaction.

BILL: I once considered marriage, but it was for a very short time. This girl and I got along very well, but I realized it was just a reaction against my father. I had dreams of going to Europe with her and just bumming around all our lives. We spent every spare minute of our time together, but she was very averse to sleeping with me. You know—the whole male thing. She'd had an unfortunate experience with her own father.

JOSÉ: Her father raped her.

BILL: It seems to me that marriage is an institution that

can't work in our society, it really can't. Each individual is just too narcissistic to accept it. At one time there was a dominant member of the family and a submissive member, but now they're too equal. They fight each other all the way. When the wife has as much say as the husband that's when the trouble comes in. Even two close friends are gonna fight like the dickens if they're on equal grounds. I think there are too many people in society today who want to be on equal grounds and can't compromise with the other guy. This is what destroyed my stepmother. She was a very aggressive, manly woman, she was a disc jockey, and she did ads on TV, she did public relations, and when my father wouldn't let her go out of the house she fought. She'd go out and do things and then come back and fight with him because he wanted home-cooking. This was all positively ridiculous, because when she would stay home, *he'd* get in the car and drive off and be gone for a whole month. Slowly, he destroyed her. He really did a job on her.

JOSÉ: In Cuba my father had a mistress.

BILL: He did?

JOSÉ: Did he ever! I found out when I was about ten. In a way I was divided about it. I thought it was terrible, but I thought it was groovy in a way. But I could understand it, even then. If it had been up to my father, what he would have done, he would have been a test pilot. He loves engines. My mother, she never stops talking.

BILL: You should see her, she goes over and sits on José's lap, and José says, Get away, get away, and she never stops.

JOSÉ: She's very afraid that I don't love her. And I

don't love her as much as I love my father. I don't want to get married with a ring and all that, you know married by Gabby Hayes as the justice of the peace, or by a horrible priest.

BILL: Marriage can be an escape from something. I had this teacher who was a pederast, and he was married and it just provided him with a human back-scratcher. And he wants to adopt kids after he's married a week. My sister married to get away from my father, I almost did. The first time she ran away from home when she was nine, because she just couldn't take it. All she's ever wanted to be was a mother. She kept trying to get pregnant from the time she was sixteen, even after all the times my mother beat her, my *real* mother. How dumb can you be? My family is the most fouled-up thing you could ever meet. My mother's a nympho, she really is, she runs around with every other man, and this man she's with now puts up with it because he loves her so much. She thinks she's Cleopatra, she really does. She says to me: I *love* the way men look at *me*. When I took José to meet her, boy, did she dress up! My sister finally latched onto this hick from Sioux City, Iowa. Every time I go there they drag out the home movies and I have to see all their home movies over and over again. My sister's enormous, she's really so fat she waddles, and she stuffs her kids. She sent me a picture of her baby and it's so fat it looks like a Mongolian idiot. They've trained their kids to beg for scraps from the table. They got three kids and want six. Every Christmas they send out a three-page mimeographed letter of what's happened to them all year. I mean they're really hicky.

JOSÉ: I don't think so. I mean, if that's your bag. I mean, you've got to have fat mothers *someplace.*

BILL: But I'm in no position to speak out to her. I'm overweight myself. But I don't know. My sister was raised by my mother, and I by my father, and when I was seven I chose to go with him. But I think I would have lost either way. My mother spent all her time going to dog shows, or to bed with men in hotel rooms. I really wanted to live with my grandfather. He pampered me, and I loved him. But my step-grandmother came between us and prevented me from living with him.

JOSÉ: That's what he really needed because his father was never home. I used to have all these fantasies about starting a dynasty. You know, getting married and getting a girl pregnant and having a kid, a replica of myself, like a toy maybe. This was when I was about seventeen. And all the kids thought that way. And a lot of them did it. But I don't think that way any more.

BILL: Ah, a family's just a business arrangement. It's gotten to the point that every time I enter the house I have to sign some legal document or another. It really is ridiculous. My family's that way. They're really very monetary. My mother's vice-president of all my father's companies which organized to beat the tax. And I'm involved because I've got stocks in all these things. Lately I started to refuse to sign all these things and my father's pulling his hair out. My father sold the house, and my mother's refused to sign the deed—and she's in the institution —she won't sign it over to him. Which means he can get arrested for breach of promise. And the people are moving in March first!

JOSÉ: The old lady's in the cage and she's holding out.
This whole country's nothing but chaos. There is
nobody to look up to. The masses need somebody to
look up to, but *me* I've got to find my *own* thing.
We can't become like our fathers.

BILL: He's very calm and ordered.

JOSÉ: I am. I am because I know who my enemy is and
I'm going to attack this. I'm going to attack this
chaotic system.

BILL: He's one of the few people I know who has security in himself. He doesn't look for somebody else
to do him favors. He'd rather do everything on his
own.

JOSÉ (laughing): It's the pioneer in me. I'm DeSoto.

BILL: I'm using José to try to get that calm and order
within myself. And he's using me because we're
dependent on each other. You know, it's gotten to
the point where you can't say you're close to
somebody or that you love somebody unless it's
somebody of the opposite sex. In this type of society
usually if you're going to have a relationship with
somebody of the opposite sex, you can't rely on
them, not the way I rely on him or he relies on me.
I depend more on him than I would depend, probably, on a wife. I couldn't depend on a wife, I can-
not conceive of it. If I married somebody it would
be because I wanted somebody around to scratch
my back and idolize me, because I've been raised
in that type of a society. But José has his art and
I have my art and we have our minds, and we sit
and we criticize each other. It's not criticism to be
destructive, but to grow. People had been lying to
us. We can say to each other that our work stinks!
Either people are afraid to tell you the truth, or

they don't know any better. Our art was stagnant for the longest time because of this.

JOSÉ: So you get to a relationship that isn't dictated, but it's on your own terms. Like with my other friends, I have to go through so much rigamarole, I have to do *their* thing.

BILL: More games! We don't regard other people's criticisms as we do each other's. It's funny, the first time I met him I thought he was a snob, and I didn't want to have anything to do with him. But we were forced to work together, and we became close. And we've known each other about seven months now.

JOSÉ: There are very few people I can talk intelligently with. It seems like it's opened up, but it's just a bigger clique. So we all got long hair. But what's that?

BILL: A relationship is like two egos coming together— you know it's like most people are so egocentric that all they want to hear is about themselves. And it's very uncommon for two egos to be compatible. It's very rare to get close to someone really. I can't stand *his* friends and he *hates* mine.

JOSÉ: The only other person we know like us is our former teacher. A really beautiful woman. She left and went to another university. But we were all very close.

BILL: Right now José and I are going down "the yellow brick road" together. If our film works out, we might stay together, if it doesn't, our egos might split apart and we'll go in different directions.

JOSEPH and JENNIFER BEAUMONT,
mid-twenties. Joseph left the priesthood and
Jennifer the nunnery; they fell in love, wrote their
own marriage ceremony, and now live in a new
apartment which they've had fun fixing up. Joseph
earns money as a social worker and Jennifer is
trying to find an active and effective role for herself
in the community. Joseph had to be at work, but the
night before the interview they agreed on what
Jennifer would relate to me about their lives.

Joseph was a priest at the parish, and I had met him a
couple of times and had talked to him. I'd also met him
at the convent at a meeting. No one is supposed to come
to these meetings late. When Joseph finally came, he
opened the door and I said, You're late and we're all
waiting for you, where have you been? And I had never
seen him before. He looked at me and said, You're
Jennifer Ann Stevens, and I said, Yeah, you must be the
new priest. He said, Yeah, I am, and I said, Oh wow!

That was our first encounter. I was a little chunky
then—my whole system had gone out of balance physically for five years. I was wrecked. I weighed 150
pounds, I had never weighed more than 120 before,
ever. Anyway, then we had a couple of liturgies at my
mother's house and I saw him. It's a kind of mass. It's
informal, and in a small group. You discuss what Chris-
tianity's all about. And you get down to kind of gutty
things—where it's at. Joseph and my mother are really
good friends.

I had been home a couple of days and I was just kind
of depressed or something, and we had all these people
and I didn't relate to anybody—so I copped out and went

to bed. We'd been having this discussion about love, and the whole thing was getting to me and I had yelled. They were talking about how to feel love for *everybody* and I was saying I don't want you to love me as *everybody*—if you can't relate to me as Jennifer, I don't want your love.

I don't usually yell at people, I'm usually very quiet and check the whole situation out and see where I fit in. But I didn't care that night, and felt that nobody cared about me. I was in a bad mood, so I went to bed. There was all this noise and then it was really quiet—and that's when the news about Kennedy being assassinated was heard. Joseph came in the bedroom and told me and it was bad.

My mother and father had been having marital troubles and when I came home from Europe, I knew it was the end and I didn't want to be around. When I first came home, my dad and I talked until about three or four o'clock in the morning, and then I decided I would go and talk to Joseph about it. He was living with this other guy that I didn't like. Joseph was sitting on the couch talking about my mom and dad—then as it happened, the rest of the evening we got talking about me, where I was and how I felt about things. He told me later that's when he really turned on to me. This was a Thursday night. And that weekend we were going to go camping. I was really kind of afraid 'cause I didn't know anybody—so the family came and all kinds of people came and that's when it all happened.

We went swimming on the little raft on the river, my brother was leading us. I felt really strange because I could never communicate or relate to anybody and I really felt isolated, but I could always communicate with Joseph. I felt he really understood me and was very perceptive. I trusted him a whole lot without knowing

him very well. So I told him that. We talked about my
mom and dad again—and he told me he really liked me
and that we had such a nice relationship because all
these women were always falling in love with him. He
liked all kinds of people and I thought he loved the
world. Well, he didn't mean that.

Joseph always knew me and knew what I was going
to say before I said it. He does that now and it's wild—
he's really perceptive—and I really trusted him. I
didn't know why, but I really trusted him. We could
really communicate. I decided I really needed to be with
him. I really like to share things with him.

We were sitting on the beach, after we had been on
the raft, and my little brother, who I really like, was
with us, and the three of us were going on this little
safari, and I said to my little brother, Hey, Robbie, how
come you didn't give me a kiss today? and he got very
embarrassed and said, Oh, no, I couldn't, and Joseph
said, Well, I haven't got mine yet either, and I said,
Okay, and it was no big deal—and then he kissed me
and I said, That was different, and he said, Well, I'm
glad you noticed. He had kissed me before and it wasn't
anything like that. Then he said, Well, did you like
it? And I said, Yeah, but you like lots of people. And he
said, It's not the same, you really turn me on, and I said,
Oh, okay. So then we were very much aware of each
other—and we sat on the beach and had this barbecue,
and I barged my way into this little space next to Joseph
and this girl who was sitting next to him nudged me with
her elbow—she wanted to sit next to him too—but I
plopped right down—and that's a lot for me to do 'cause
I usually don't do those kinds of things. So I just kind of
poked her in the eye and she fell over. And then we ate
and sang songs underneath the stars.

Joseph was going to sleep on the boat. These other kids said they would go get the bunks ready—so I said, Okay. They said they would call me when everything was ready. We were sitting there and it was taking them an awful long time—it was so quiet. We were talking, and I snuggled up next to Joseph, and he gave me this big, fat kiss and I didn't know what to do with it. It's funny we were talking about this last night—kind of reliving the whole thing—and we were saying, I'll be you and you'll be me. I wanted Joseph to show me how I was that night. So we reversed roles. We did it—it was really funny.

He told me how I turned him on the first time we went out when my watch got caught on my nylons, and he came over to help me get it out. He said he was really uptight the first time he got turned on to me because he didn't know what to do about his vows and things. He wasn't worried—I don't think he ever worries about anything. He's one of the most free people I've ever met—where it comes from inside free. But he hadn't felt those things before about anybody and he knew all kinds of people. Women were very attracted to him—but he had never felt deep love about anybody. So he had all these feelings and didn't know what to do with them, or what they meant. And he never missed anybody like he missed me. I mean he could be with people and he could not be with people and it was okay. So he went to Europe not knowing what it was with me. Or what it meant—but he had strong feelings.

My mother saw what was happening on that week-end camp-out. It was really fantastic, because she didn't know what he would do with his priesthood. Joseph went to Europe in the middle of the summer, and it wasn't until he came back that he decided that he loved me. He didn't know what was happening, but he really missed me when he was in Europe. He'd been held back twice from his ordination because he was a rebel. He didn't like people in authority. He just did his thing and so they held him back twice. He would have made the decision very soon anyway, to leave the priesthood, so I just brought it about more quickly.

Joseph has been suspended and excommunicated from the Roman Church since he married me. We're both excommunicated. My mother was worried that I couldn't take communion—and I said, Who's going to know—or who cares?

To be excommunicated doesn't mean anything. You don't get a letter or anything. My mother had gone through my struggles for two years with me about the convent, and she knew that this is what I wanted to do. But she was sick, physically ill with the whole thing. Not so much me, but Joseph—suspended! What's happened to the Church? For me, the suspension was easier because I had just temporary vows. Joseph's were not. Mine had run out and I had not renewed them.

We slept together before we married—in my parents' house. And my father was home. I got so uptight—I wanted Joseph to go for a walk outside. I didn't feel good about going to bed with him until we got married. I guess I was never in love before Joseph.

We got married in a Methodist church, with the congregation full of Jews and Protestants and atheists.

BERNADETTE CLOSYNSKI, in her mid-fifties, lives in a middle-sized city in Connecticut. She loves her husband very much and spends long hours with him out in his boat fishing in Long Island Sound. For a happy marriage she says a woman must give up "a mind of her own."

I've been married twenty-two years and marriage between my husband and I is a fifty-fifty proposition. Neither one of us makes a decision without consulting the other and this is the way I think a marriage should be. We've had a very happy, successful marriage. We very seldom argue. My husband has a hobby of fishing, so I have adopted his hobby. He and I go out in his boat, we go out on the river and we sit there for hours on end. We say a few words to each other, discuss a few problems at home—once in a while if I'm not catching the fish and he should hook one, he hands the rod to me so I can reel it in.

This is a happy marriage too because I let him think he is the boss and he knows that I let him think he is the boss. But then if he wants to do something, I will go along with it. I have a man who works hard all day long, he's a construction electrician. He comes home, he would like to go fishing, so instead of his asking me, I'll suggest to him. After twenty-two years, I can read his mind. So I say to him, Why don't you go fishing tonight, Ray? See?

Now three quarters of your electricians before they come home go into a bar-room to have a few beers. They don't show up until seven, seven-thirty. My husband, he finishes work at four-thirty, he's close by, he calls here at twenty-five minutes to five.

He was a Coast Guardsman and he was a roller-skating addict like myself and I was introduced to him in a roller-skating rink called the Chez Rue in Boston. He asked me to go out with him, I went out with him. I had been engaged twice previously but my mother always pointed out what was wrong with this person I was engaged to and eventually I saw that she was right; she was a very smart woman. She had a high degree of ESP, very, very, and she was psychic—only she didn't recognize what it was. In those days I never knew what it was, but now I know.

My mother called me up at a quarter of six one morning, crying her eyes out, and she called to me, Why didn't you tell me your baby girl was dead? I was to go into the hospital that morning to give birth, eight years ago, to a baby, and I knew the baby was dead, its life had ceased the day before, yet my mother knew what sex the child was, and sure enough, at quarter of six that evening I gave birth to a stillborn baby girl.

I don't believe in trial marriage because I'm moral—I'm old-fashioned. I was brought up strict and very old-fashioned and I believe in sex in marriage. Sex before marriage I don't believe in. I know youngsters do it today, I know this, but I don't believe in trial marriages.

I've got two nice children. They're old enough to know better now. I hope they have taken up the example of their father and I, but of course they do have their own lives to live.

My daughter is stubborn—very hard-headed—she has a mind of her own. A woman who enters marriage should forget that mind of her own. In my family, we were never allowed to argue—we were generally home and it was kept clean by we three girls and my mother —my brothers never had to do anything. We three—

the four of us did it—females. When my older brothers would argue, my mother would step in, and no matter how old they were, they had to kiss each other. And if you saw two men kissing each other on the cheek, they started to laugh—all anger was forgotten, no arguments. See my mother—she was the eldest of seven girls in Ireland—my grandfather never had a son, that's bad, because my mother naturally inherited all the property and she signed it over to her sisters. Girls had to do everything in that family, so we had to do everything. We had to learn to cook when we were eleven years of age.

My father never laid a hand on my mother, never laid a hand on her, that's the truth—in all the years. My mother was the one who gave us a slap, but my father never laid a hand on us. He was too gentle a man. But my mother ruled the roost—she had to, someone had to rule it. When you have a man who's gentle and mild like that, someone must rule the roost, especially when there's ten children in that home.

My husband is the type who doesn't care to embarrass his children, but don't ever think he's too gentle. I mean he has red hair and he is—they call him Red. We have a happy marriage, very happy for twenty-two years. If I had to do it all over again, I'd do it. There are men in this world, let's be honest, that to me they're men, period; they hold no attraction to me and this is the God's honest truth, and as long as I know this man, he's the only one I know. He feels the same way, too.

Now I send him up to the Cape with his brother and a friend for four days. Once a year I do that. They go fishing; they would like to catch that big, big, big, big one, that fifty-five or sixty-pound one. How many times have I gone camping with him? I'd be up all night

sitting on the bank of the canal while he's down there
fishing for that big one and I'd be freezing because it
goes down into the forties even in midsummer. But we
enjoy ourselves. I hope you will be as fortunate as he
and I.

**STEVEN WESTERSON, an electronics salesman
in his early thirties, lives in a middle-sized town in
the Midwest. He is extremely involved in his work
and spends most of his free time working on
inventions combining sound, images, and lighting
effects in a total environment. He's lately been
dieting to make himself more attractive because
he wants to fall in love. He hopes he's met the right
man at last.**

I'd only met him briefly once before, and this night we
suddenly felt so close—I said to him, Look, when you
look at me—I felt unusually close to him (I'm usually
sort of reticent, especially in anything that resembles
a romantic situation); we were getting close to each
other, we hadn't gone to bed together . . . I just felt
strong contact, stronger than I usually feel . . . with
somebody I don't know much—I said, When you look
at me, what do you see? Who do you see? So he said, I
see these two eyes, I see these two legs, I see . . . some
people don't have a nose, some people don't have a chin,
and then he said, I don't have a future.

And I said, What do you mean?

He said, I just came back from Europe where I went
for two weeks to say good-bye to my family. I have
leukemia. Two years ago the doctor told me I had two

and a half or three years to live, but now the time is
getting short. So he told his family and the man he's
been living with.

First of all I was attracted to him, but now I sort of
identified with him, because I've been like that since I
was six. But I've always been living with the idea that
I've got six years, seven years. But there's something different between that and six months. It always seems far
off to me, because when I lived past twelve I felt tri-
umphant, now I feel like I might have ten years left.
That's not being optimistic, but realistic.

I'm prepared to move in with him. I feel open to
him. I said to him, I want to make a bargain with you.
I'm available to you and you call me when you want.
And he said, Okay. We still didn't go to bed together,
but it didn't matter whether we did or not because we
were that close, both physically and emotionally. I don't
know what happened that night, but we couldn't separate, we couldn't get out of this place where we had
dinner, we couldn't separate, we were holding on somehow.

Among the bits of information he did know about
me, he did know about my heart, he said. It must be sort
of public information. He told me he wasn't close to his
friend whom he lived with the way he felt with me. I
felt and feel completely vulnerable to him, but I don't
want to rush him, and I want him to understand that. I
know he understands that I was deeply involved with
him on that occasion.

I don't know to what degree the circumstances make
me vulnerable to him, I don't know. He is the one that
I look at, the one who talks like he talks, and this one
has no future. To me, he's both himself and his condition. Can't separate them at all. I like his soul and he

looks nice, but that isn't what knocks me out. Oh, he's handsome, but that isn't the starting point.

He hasn't called me yet. Thursday night it felt like already a year. I said to myself, I know he'll call this morning. We have a dinner date for next Wednesday, but it's with the man he lives with too.

The way he talks is very extraordinary, because he doesn't have the time. Things are all packed together in a completely logical way, which he apologized for at one point. Everything's essential. He said he just can't put in the time to link it all, and I said, Fine.

I haven't been in love for a long time. Part of that is deliberate. I haven't wanted to have that feeling with anyone. For one thing I can't stand the endings. It was so difficult, the second love affair that I ever had, I collapsed when it ended; I really did. That's when I had to go to the shrink. I'd stopped talking altogether. I was always afraid, though, that this particular guy was going to leave me. I used to play games with him. I'd ask him, like every day and a half, Are you thinking of cutting out? I had such a terrible opinion of myself, I couldn't understand why anyone should have good feelings toward me. I felt that if anyone came to know me the illusion would be shattered. That I had gotten by somehow, by playing a role.

I watched this poor guy like a hawk, it was obsessive and took so much energy. At one point I got sick and went to the hospital to some ward. And he didn't visit me at all. I'd go to the phone booth and call him up and he'd be so cold. When I got out I kept pumping and pumping him: Did you see anybody; and who were you with? He kept saying, Nobody, nothing; but then one day he did say he'd seen someone. Of course, it was evidence then to back up my obsessions.

After that, of course, the first time I went to bed with this girl, she got pregnant. I was twenty-one. She and I went through a very very intense time together. We liked each other. I knew that she knew I was living with this guy. I tried to keep it from her that I was living with this guy, it was just at the end of the affair. Then I got very very physically sick and I told her about this guy, and she was miserable to learn that the relationship with the guy had been what it was. When I went to bed with her it was almost over with this guy, and I felt so despairing . . . I moved in with my sister and stayed on her davenport and I wasn't talking to anybody. Then the girl came to visit me one day there and she told me she was pregnant.

She wanted to know what to do, should we get married or what, and I said, No. But I took her to my shrink and he said we shouldn't get married and he was right. I felt responsible for her and not only that, some part of me, like the way a person likes Christmas even though it's vulgarized and commercialized, a part of me thought that marriage was really a nice thing. I'd like to have that wedding picture of me in my head with me as a groom.

But we went to another state and got her an abortion. It was very very expensive, my sister paid for it. It was terrible. My sister had to hold her and kiss her and virtually lay on top of her while the guy was operating. The doctor didn't give her any anesthetic.

All this time, I'm so obsessed with this guy, and the shrink was saying to me, You're looking at him like a sailboat, where you could see a beautiful white sail from a distance, but if you came up close the sail wouldn't be so white. I'd had one crush on a guy before that, but I hadn't had anything like this before. I hadn't ever been in love with a girl either.

I lived in Florida for a while, where my parents had sent me to a child cardiac home, a charity home. It was in Miami and it was very sunny, and that was the main point, that it was good for my condition. When first there, you're put in solitary for a few months. I told my parents I didn't want to go. They said if I didn't like it I could come back in three weeks. So the days were very, very long. I counted the days like anything. At the end of three weeks I said, I hate it, I can't stand it. They said, You have to stay three weeks anyway. We were very poor. I'd spent the first time I had this condition in bed at home because we couldn't afford a hospital. For a year and a half I stayed in the living room. We had three rooms and eight people living in them. I had to stay there without moving, while my mother is taking the bedpan back and forth. I had to stay there day and night without moving. The first time my illness hit, it was terrible, because I was torn away from my little five- and six-year-old friends, and made to lay down there. You don't feel like laying down without moving when you're six. They took away my shoes, and they said the reason I had to stay in bed was that I needed new shoes, and when they gave me new shoes I could get up. I bought it, but I said, I'd go without shoes, but they said I couldn't.

In the home I was only seen by a doctor and a nurse for the first two and a half months, then they put me into a room with two other guys. We were allowed a little time in the wheelchair each day, the rest of the time we had to lay down. Pretty soon I got up. I remember learning masturbation in that room with the other two guys. We admitted to each other that we were all in some way doing it, then we got to talking about it, and then we got to doing it, then we got to talking about it, and then we got to doing it openly, when we were sure no one was looking in the window, the nurse or the orderlies. Then we decided it was bad for us and that we'd have to stop. We decided that that may have been the cause of our heart condition. We knew we masturbated and we knew we had heart conditions. I don't know what made us convinced that masturbation was bad, but we were quite convinced of it. We had this calendar where we marked off the days that we didn't masturbate. One guy couldn't keep from it. He decided he didn't want to deprive himself of it, but the other two of us lied. I lied, I remember, about the number of times. I admitted to having done it, but I tried to make it an "acceptable" number. (Laughs)

But soon I got moved to another house and got to go to school. They gave me a job that excited me, I got to mimeograph. Everyone there had a mock marriage. Everyone there had a wife or husband AND child. The child was a little kid that you adopted. I had a wife. We had a little marriage ceremony, I remember, with my wife, already being very, very jealous when I heard that somebody had kissed her. To kiss somebody on the cheek, mind you, was as far as you went. Anybody could pick anybody, we'd eat together, we'd play together.

I'd been writing my family all this time, telling them, I hate it, I can't stand it. Just as I got adjusted, my family decided to let me come home. I was ambulatory. I had a wife, I had a kid, I had a job at school, I was walking to school. I was in the most advanced state of animation that you could be in and still be at this place. It was fun by that point. The doctor said to me, Your family wants you home, but I think you should stay at least two months more, but I said, No, I want to go home if they want me. But part of me really didn't. I wanted to go because I'd been waiting for a long time for them to say, Okay, now you can come home. But at that point I really didn't.

So I went to them, but in the meantime, they'd moved. It was from Miami to Kansas City. I didn't know anybody; I didn't know my family, I didn't know my mother or my sister or my brother. They were all strangers. They couldn't have been more strangers to me. They were acting like "family" and I was acting like "son" and "brother." I never believed for a minute we were anything that we were playing, never!

We all knew when my parents made it together, because my mother hated it so. She hated him so. I still don't know who was the instigator of that horror between them, but I do know they couldn't stand each other. We'd arrive for breakfast in the morning, and there she'd be, having special antagonism to him, a special new wave of contempt for him. He had brutalized her, he had had his way.

Once I discovered rubbers in their drawer and I knew it had something to do with the sexual act. I somehow put it together, with information from my friends, and what I could see between them. They were caught up in this misery together, all the problems of poverty, day after day after day, of eight of us in this dreary room, of one of us never moving. I think that my leaving was just another trauma to my mother.

I don't know how it all started, but according to my mother she was a raving beauty, and something of a terrific singer, and she sang in a sort of nightclub, where my father went to admire her. Now her father, according to her, was some sort of paragon of virtue. He was as high as you could get on the virtue ladder. Anyway my parents married and came to this country. She had a little boy, but began to miss her father terribly. My father got so he couldn't stand her and he kicked her out. So she took her little boy and got on a boat to Europe and she was pregnant. After a while her father wrote to her husband to please take her back, that another child had been born. In the meantime the first baby had died, and she would never tell my father about it.

Anyway, my mother comes home and my father accuses her of killing the first baby. She explained that the baby died from drinking raw milk, but he accused her of killing it through neglect and something else. One night, vocally, in front of all of us he accused her of killing the first son.

They never, in all my life, did anything but hate each other.

On his death bed, he was asking for her and she wouldn't come. And yet their relationship was very intense, because of forty years living together with all that hatred. My younger sister and I would go to see him on alternating days. He was dying. On one day that she was there the doctor said he wouldn't survive unless he had this tracheotomy, so she signed for him to have it. She waited outside. She goes in the room and asks the doctor, How is he? He's fine. She finds him like this, with his throat open. They didn't give him an anesthetic or anything to ease the pain, and they tied his hands down. My sister and I decided at a certain point that they should let him die. We went to the doctor and asked him to let him die. He said no. I asked if there was any chance for survival. He said, First of all, one can never say no, but I would say it is 99 percent that he won't survive.

My father had stopped seeing, he'd stopped hearing. He tried to talk but he couldn't. The doctor said everything was sterilized because the slightest infection would do him in. So one day, my sister and I went to visit our father, and I took my spit and put it in his mouth. The next day he was dead.

ERIC LINDQUIST, fifty-eight, is a Pacific Northwest salmon fisherman. Eric is another old friend of mine. He and George Almquist and I fished off log booms together when I was a teen-ager. He loves to "needle" people and give advice.

My friend Guy was always a rabble-rouser. He was raised over east of the mountains, raised up in what they call a chumpstick. This was people who went over there during the Depression and just like squatted. They built up sod huts and that kind of stuff and that's the way they lived. Anyhow he comes to Seattle and he meets this Louise and they got married. Well, this guy Guy he was a rounder: he'd be in one night and out the other. He was trying to make a couple of bucks any way he could and she was a bookkeeper. Sometimes he'd be over in the chumpstick for a couple of months at a time picking apples, and they never did have any children. Anyhow, he comes dragging this gal in one night—this Joanne, and he tells Louise, Well, here we are. I got her pregnant, and I can't afford an abortion, and do you want to pay for it? And she says, No, I'll be damned if I'll pay for an abortion! Well, he says, I guess I'm stuck then, I haven't got the money. She says, Well, I don't know about you, Guy, but I'll pay for the whole kaboodle if she has the kid. So Joanne goes to the hospital and has the baby, so when she has the baby, she's got no place to go, so Louise says, Well, bring her home.

They set up a whole big deal down in their basement, and that's where Joanne and the baby stayed. Joanne would do the dishes and all the housework while Louise was working, so anyhow that's where this girl was raised up.

Well, all four of them used to go out on weekends. Louise bought this camper for them and they'd go over east of the mountains and pick mushrooms. Louise and Guy'd been married for twenty years, and Louise just accepted it for what it was. She said, Guy's a donkey. And anyway she was the boss. Jesus, she was the boss of the whole outfit. She raised up that little girl. Whatever Louise said to the rest of them they did. That's right! Because she bought the camper and set up the whole kaboodle. She was like that old gal in the book *Hawaii*, she was the boss. She didn't drink, but she was the boss and what she said went.

So anyhow, they're over there east of the mountains picking mushrooms and they come back down off the pass, and Louise gets a heart attack. By the time they come down from the mountains she's had it. I went in and talked to her at the hospital the night before she died, she was a wonderful person, but she knew she'd had it.

Well, all this time the four of them was living together Joanne was resenting Louise, because she was in love with Guy. But she didn't dare say anything, because Louise was the boss. She told them what to do and she told the kid what to do. And the kid was a pretty good kid till Louise died. Then the kid started telling everyone what to do. I've sat there and heard the kid's own mother telling her, when the kid is acting up: You wouldn't say that if Louise was still around!

Well, it's five years since Louise died. Now all this time Joanne had been bugging Guy to get married. And he don't want to. He's telling me all the time, Jesus I hate to do it. And he asks me to be his best man, but I says, Not if you feel that way about it, fella.

This son of a bitch doesn't want to marry her because Joanne gets about four hundred bucks a month from this Aid to Dependent Children. He's retired, on Social Security. Now if he marries Joanne and the government finds out they've been taking them for this ADC and that kind of stuff—Jesus! In the meantime the kid don't even know that Guy's her father. She calls him Guy. If they found out, the state would crucify him.

Of course, this kid's a little blabbermouth. One time when she was about five or six, I come down to their house and she starts whispering and yakketyyakking at me, and she says to me, Guess what? Last night Guy come downstairs and went to bed with my mother. This kid's a little blabbermouth, y'see.

Well, Guy's mellowed a lot in the last ten years. His only problem is to try to figure out how to tell the kid that he's her real father.

MARY JANE DONOHUE, in her early sixties, is an old drinking buddy of Eric's and George's. She's worked many years as a florist, but now baby-sits to pick up spare change. She's the shuffleboard champion of the Midget Tavern. She bets on herself and that's where she makes her "real" money.

I adored my in-laws, they were my second mother and father. Poor Mom. The last few years she was alive, she just couldn't wait till I came to see her. I'd fix her face and do her hair, she wouldn't let anybody else touch her hair. My first husband couldn't stand how close we were, but that was the way it was. His folks loved me, and they loved me till they died.

My sister-in-law sure fouled up with her kids. She used to look down her nose at me, but now she's got her arms full of trouble. Her two youngest kids come to me when they're in trouble or when they're happy. You got to let kids do what they want to do. You can't tell them what to do, you got to help them. Now I could have taken a job a year ago, before my son-in-law died. I could have had a good job and got lost from this whole country. But I was meant to stay here because my daughter needed me as it turned out.

When my mother died I used to pray every night that I'd live long enough to be able to raise my two daughters. I prayed every night to my mother, not to God. Well, then it turned out that both my children got well situated, and now I'm putting the pressure on the Lord because I want to *see* my *great*-grandchildren. So this is what I do, I demand, I demand all the time. This is the way I am.

I was a beautiful grandmother for a while, but I just couldn't fit that picture. I been trying to be anybody but me. I'm Mary Jane Donohue! I came from a big family. Thirteen brothers and sisters, I was the baby. I don't know how to be a mother, I don't know how to be a grandmother, but I know how to be a little sister. That's what I'm best at.

Once we tried the owning-our-own-home shit, but only once, that was enough for me. People ask me why we don't own our own home. I tried it. I raised chickens. Is was a beautiful acre and a half that we could have made into a beautiful park, BUT—my husband wouldn't come home, and I got stuck there. He stopped in the beer parlor every night after work. That's all he could think about. He didn't want to come home and do any work, so you know who shoveled the chicken shit? Me. And I was working as a waitress all day long, I come home and fed the chickens, I put in any flowers that we had—I loved doing it, but I wanted somebody to come home and be with me at night.

There was this one tavern on the way home that he just couldn't get by. He'd stay there and play shuffle-board and come home at twelve or one o'clock. Half the time I'm taking care of his son, and his son didn't want a stepmother. So once a week I'd have to shovel the shit out of the chicken house. He never cleaned it once. I loved this place, I really loved it. But anyhow, when the roof started to leak and he didn't fix it, and he didn't put in the carport—I said this is it. When he didn't fix the leak in my roof, I says, To hell with you! I put up with that for three and a half years, but the leak in the roof did it. I says, I'm moving out today, I don't care where you're going. So we moved back to town and started renting again. He wasn't even making the payments on the house, I was.

We don't make any more joint decisions in this house. I got a bank account and he's got a bank account. What I spend on household, he has to pay me back. You know why he did this to me? Because I screwed his ex-wife's husband. That's when he took everything away. He set up the separate bank accounts then.

MARGARET and SAMUEL, a couple in their early
thirties, have just married. The only time they leave
each other is to go to work. When at home or
entertaining, they are always close, holding each
other, or holding hands, or gazing at one another
with unconditional approval. They try to include
anyone who visits in this love. They really feel
lucky to have found each other.

MARGARET: I was like twenty-nine when I met Samuel,
I was old. And I've met so many kooks—after you're
twenty-five, a lot of men you date are of a certain
kind. They either want to sleep with you or they're
kooks—they have really odd hangups. And so you
have this constant problem. Because of my religious
background, I couldn't have slept with them even
if I had wanted to. When I would kiss someone I
would even feel guilty because of my background.
I would feel like I was wicked—like I was evil—as
if I had robbed a bank. Like if you copied in school
and the teacher caught you and scolded you. I felt
the same kind of guilt. I never kissed anyone without feeling guilt except for Samuel. He was the first
one. I had a lot of these guilt feelings I shouldn't
have. I was thinking I had to suffer in order to be
righteous.—We met on the Long Island Railroad.

SAMUEL: I was reading the newspaper.

MARGARET: What happened was that he had the theatri-
cal page, and I asked him if he was interested in the
theater, and he told me yes, he wanted to be a producer and I said, Oh, that was interesting and I
said, Have you ever been to La Mama's.

SAMUEL: Yeah, that was the thing with the big clique.

MARGARET: I had been to La Mama's one time. And I thought I knew the theater then, because I thought I was really in. I had seen about six plays, that's all I'd ever seen. But I started discussing everything I had ever seen, because he was so sophisticated and I felt so ill at ease sitting there. He had on this beret and sunglasses, and this safari jacket—and then I forgot about him.

SAMUEL: I told her I had invested in *Tom Paine*, and eventually I wanted to be a producer. And she was the first woman I had ever met who had gone down to La Mama on her own. Then I saw her at the beach.

MARGARET: That afternoon I was sitting with my friends, and he came up to where I was sitting and he kept rubbing my leg. He was a very fresh man. And you were the first person that ever did something like that. And then he gave me a calling card.

SAMUEL: Just a card with my name on it and a phone number.

MARGARET: And then my date made me bury it in the sand, 'cause he didn't want me to see him. George didn't notice him rubbing my leg, 'cause it wasn't that obvious to anyone else. And Sam didn't even remember rubbing my leg. But it shook me up. Like if someone was heavily petting you.

SAMUEL: It was very erotic to her.

MARGARET: It really shook me up. So when George saw I was all engrossed with him, he made me bury the card. So when he went to the latrine I dug it up and put it down my bathing suit. So finally I called him, and he said he was going to the park and I could

come for a walk. And so I went for a walk in the
park with him. I wasn't scared to see him. The reason I went was because I was mad at George, and
the first time I was with Sam, I just never felt that
he could like me. I always figured he had a hundred
and one girls.

SAMUEL: Oh, God.

MARGARET: So I met him, and he was all dressed in black
with a green scarf.

SAMUEL: I was delighted. I thought, well, finally one of
those cards had paid off. My mother printed the
cards for me. My mother wanted me to be married
—she's a good Jewish mother.

MARGARET: They were just business cards.

SAMUEL: Personal cards. She was the first woman who
really ever called. And I had a great deal of respect
for her because she took the initiative. So many
women are under the impression that they have to
do only certain kinds of things.

MARGARET: And that's the kind of woman I was.

SAMUEL: And it's great for a woman to be a man's equal.
They should be able to call and say, Hi, what are
you doing, and so on and so forth. This is what I
felt. You know, a great many women, or I should
say girls, don't take any initiative. They're not
human beings. They should be equal. The only real
difference between a man and a woman is that
a woman has the ability to bear children. And I
thought it was so wonderful of her to call me. Somebody had enough balls, guts, whatever you want to
call it to call. To say what are you doing. And I said
I was going to the park, and do you want to come
along? We met in front of my house.

MARGARET: I picked him up at his door.

SAMUEL: And we went over to the park, and I took her on a boat ride.

MARGARET: He did the whole romantic bit—I was just flabbergasted 'cause he had wine and cheese.

SAMUEL: You know, there was a restaurant in the park, and we picked up these things. It's outdoors by a fountain, and we sat there and watched all the people go by and drank the wine and ate the cheese and talked. And afterwards we walked by the zoo, and came back across the Sheep Meadow, and I gave her a very big kiss.

MARGARET: He gave me the first French kiss I ever had. In the South, rowing in Central Park is considered a great romantic thing. So when he took me rowing I felt like he was very suave. I didn't feel he was doing it to make an impression on me or to be extra nice to me, I just felt he was very suave and always took women rowing. And I associated wine and cheese with Italian Romeos. And then when he kissed me I knew he was Mr. Suave. The Sunday night date I had with him, he kept saying to me, Go home early, because I lived way out on the Island; and I thought he wanted me to go home because his wife was coming.

SAMUEL: In my place, a wife?

MARGARET: 'Cause your house was so clean, I knew you must be married. And really his house is clean 'cause he's immaculate. But in my mind I thought he must be married. I just felt probably he would never date me again.

SAMUEL: When I told her to go home early, I was seriously concerned about the long trip out there.

MARGARET: So I saw him again, because he phoned me, I had given him my number. And then he dated me every Saturday and Sunday for one year. My mother decided she was going back to Miami and we really never *decided* to get married, did we?

SAMUEL: It wasn't your decision.

MARGARET: I never decided.

SAMUEL: I finally told her mother, Margaret and I are going to get married, I love her. I told her mother first.

MARGARET: It was a Monday night, and my mother was here as a tourist. Samuel wanted to take her out, and she didn't want to go out 'cause she's a very temperamental person, she wants a lot of attention. And she thought she was getting more attention by staying home in bed being too tired or slightly sick than she would get by going out. It's a little weird. So I had a fight with her over it, and I got very upset.

SAMUEL: Her mother would start piling on the guilt feelings, she really just broke her down. I remember, I came into the hotel room, I was going to take them both out to eat, and so a whole scene, I mean you're in New York—a tourist. And she was sitting in a corner of the bathroom and she had tears rolling down her eyes and her mother was in there and she was carrying on, and she was packed to go home.

MARGARET: So Samuel sat down on the bed and said, You can't go home now, because we're getting married Friday. And so my mother looked at me and said, Is that true? And before I could say I don't know, he said, Will you marry me Friday? So she went to bed, and she said we should go out, so we went to the restaurant, and we stole eighteen pieces of sugar because that's a good luck number.

SAMUEL: Eighteen is a symbol in the Hebrew alphabet.

You see a lot of Jewish women wear this symbol. It means life. It's the eighteenth letter.

MARGARET: Samuel makes the decisions in our marriage.

SAMUEL: Oh, God, we both make decisions.

MARGARET: But we agree, we're very compatible, really. I would say we're usually compatible. He's the only person in the whole world that I have ever been able to live with easily. He's not even frustrated.

SAMUEL: Why do you think I married her? I didn't marry her to make me feel more masculine, I wanted the woman I married to be completely independent. That's the whole point. She can take care of herself.

MARGARET: I married him because I really enjoy him. And because he's always so beautiful to me and so kind. I would like children if they could be duplicates of Samuel. I want them to have the same little curls that Samuel has. The barber tries to straighten Samuel's curls, but I won't let him.

SAMUEL: We would probably have one child.

MARGARET: If he comes out just like you.

SAMUEL: It could be a girl.

MARGARET: Oh, I would keep her if she was a girl.

SAMUEL: What do you mean, *you'll keep* her? What would you do, throw her out in the street?

MARGARET: I want to become a sculptor. You know why? Because his body is so beautiful, I want to copy it.

SAMUEL: According to her, I have a great back.

MARGARET: He does. It's just gorgeous. It turns me on, but artistically it's just beautiful. I've seen other people's sculptured bodies in museums. And I would like him for a model. But I wouldn't like everyone to see him that I know. So I just want the backside.

SAMUEL: Any time.

DONALD CORNELL, a quiet businessman in his early fifties, has been a widower for several years. His mother is raising his children. He has no intentions of marrying again.

My wife died ten years ago. In this country here marriage isn't an easy deal, it's a two-way street, you have to work at it. I've never met anyone since, where the situation could develop again. My parents stayed together all their lives, they had a pretty good thing going for them. I have two boys, but they don't live with me. I don't see them too often. They'd rather be with my mother. I have nothing to say about what they do. I feel I'd like to sometimes, but it's better that they do whatever they do. It's easier on them to be with her.

I have very little rapport with that situation. I get angry about it sometimes, but as long as I send the old green stuff in there, things seem to go along pretty well.

I think it's important for a lot of people to be married, it helps in business. But it hasn't held me back, since I'm not counting on going too far. It's important for these people who set their lives on their jobs, but for me I'm taking it easy. Marriage is a tough deal. You know, a wife's like a subway, if you don't have the coin you don't ride the machine. Ya got to have the loot. You can't buy a newspaper if you can't pay for it. Same thing with a wife. If you don't have that green stuff, you might as well pack it in. Finance is very important if you're going to have a wife.

I thought when I had my wife things were going pretty good toward my way, but it all gets like a habit. I thought I was in love when I got married, I got what I anticipated, what I had was very nice, but I don't think

I'd go into it again. I don't ever want to be obligated
again. You got people depending on you. You got to
think about their feelings and their needs. You lose all
your own importance. You always got to report in. Marriage is a great thing though!

I think marriage should be a fifty-fifty deal. The wife
shouldn't work, she should remain a feminine person and
dress up and so on. Now I've found in my lifetime that
the female is so attractive to the male—that women are
intelligent, but they hold it back. They always understand any situation better than the men. They usually
know how to do things better. They don't come right out
with it, but they always make you feel a little inferior.
I'm sure if a woman ran for President most everybody
would vote for her. Women are very sincere people and
this is what this country needs. We're going backwards,
and a woman is what this country needs. They've tried
the rest—right—why don't they try the best—right? In
my lifetime I've met a lot of fine women, and I say this
with all due respect, I've yet to find one woman who
didn't have more mentality than all the men I know.
They seem to have this living desire, but somebody's got
to tap it. We're all way off base. We should send a
couple of these smart girls over to Asia and straighten
it all out. I don't have very many close friends. It's a
question that you can only be good to a certain amount
of people. I don't think that the way I move around, that
you can really acquire too many friends; if you do, it's
very rare. I'm pretty much of a loner.

I'm not even close to my company. I feel that if I do
my job, that's about all I can do. I can't set the world on
fire. Now what I really like, I like politics. Like this
fella Nixon. I want to see him really do the right thing.
In my lifetime now I'd like to see this fella Nixon ship

the green stuff to those guys in Asia and put a stop to all the mess and get this country on the right road. All you have to do is call up the key men. Call up Khrushchev, or whoever's over there in China and say, All right, how much you guys need for us to have a little peace here? All it takes is dollars. Just send the dollars over, make the deal, and he'd make himself a big guy in this country. He's got to come up with the loot.

I was my father's shadow, I was his favorite and I always looked up to him. My mother is very smart, this is what people tell me, and I believe it. But Joyce Brothers, I think she's the sweetest—I'm telling you about a brain—that is a brain. I was at a company seminar with her, and you should have seen her straighten out these guys. Boy, is she logical. She can straighten anybody out. And this is what this country needs, logic and reason, and leadership. John Kennedy had this, but they didn't give him a chance! He had everything going for him— what a guy!

Younger people need somebody to look up to, but who we got in this country? All right, Nixon's a businessman, but the young guys need something else, they need somebody! What ya gonna do? All I know, it's a big country. But I got some good advice for young people— it's this. It's the same advice that I received from my father when I was about fifteen years old: Donald, he said, I'll never see you again—he was one of the top guys on the East Coast—he says, Always do the right thing, because the good guys win out in the end. I never forgot it.

SISTER CECILIA is a member of a convent strug-
gling to find a relevant way to live and act within the
larger community while still maintaining itself as a
religious community. She is forty, holds a Ph.D., and
earns money teaching college. Half her salary goes
to the mother house for communal needs.

When I was a real young kid I just had a yen to do
something significant with my life. All kids who go to
nuns' schools think about being a nun for a time. My
folks didn't want me to be a nun. My father wanted me
to be in the theater—he thought about the theater the
way other people thought about the Church. He was a
great romantic about it, and when I was a little kid he
dragged me to it all the time. He'd talk to me about
Margaret Sullavan and Katharine Cornell as if they were
saints. But in the course of going to Catholic schools I
met some marvelous women—they were mind-stretching
women; they were valiant and they were women I
wanted to be like. They were the only people I'd met in
my life that were of that stature. They felt to me like
they were tremendously free. They weren't caught up
with whether they had a new car. They weren't caught
up with what they wore—they really weren't caught up
with themselves—they were very wide-minded. It just
seemed to me it would be a great thing to be so self-
extending. They had vision, they made you feel like you
could get out there and really become bigger.

   Our present Mother General—a woman of sixty—
you can still look at this woman and think she's extraordinary.

   It was a struggle for me, I also wanted other things
—I wanted to go into the theater—I thought you could

stretch yourself by getting inside another character. But one day right in the middle of a play I decided that theater isn't God, it's not absolute, and people all around me were treating it as if it were a temple—but I just decided it wasn't enough.

But now I'm much older and I still don't know what God is. I've been in love twice. Once I almost went ahead and got married and I think I would have had a perfectly lovely life. I still think that particular fellow and I could have managed to survive. Nothing stopped it, but I'd go past a church and I'd go in and pray, at the same time I was doing another thing at night. Young kids today have many more options open to them. The world was different then. Nowadays, kids can join the Peace Corps, the underground church, and so on. Now this makes us ask ourselves whether or not our historical usefulness is over, whether or not this thing served its purpose in its time and—the question is where to go and in which direction, and that's the anxiety of the moment.

When I entered the order I thought it would be a meaningful way to spend my time. I really didn't think the habit would last more than a year even then. I didn't enter the Church for security. I was secure with my folks, I had a guy, I would have been reasonably secure if I got married. I had a job, I was earning pretty good money—it wasn't a conscious search for security. After I'd been in a year, they sent around a questionnaire asking us why we'd come, and I couldn't answer a single question. I wasn't a little girl when I went in, I was twenty-three and I didn't feel like a little girl. There were kids in there with me who were seventeen and who were grown up and there were kids in there who were seventeen and who were little girls. For one thing, I didn't do it right away. My mother was opposed to it, she wept. She was never angry, she was only saddened —she thought it was unnatural. And it is unnatural! The natural thing was to get married and have grandchildren. If I'd become a suburban housewife and had children she could play with forever, she'd have been happy.

But when I look back on my life things have *happened* to me. Things have happened to me that wouldn't have happened if I'd gone off and married this guy. Neither one of my parents is stupid, and the older I get the more authentic I find them. My mother went through real grief—she told me it was just like dying. I grew up in a house with terrific parental love. I don't have this thing some of my poor kids have, parents who don't care. This is one of my basic foundations. I've met *their* parents, and they just don't care.

One of my biggest struggles when I went through the novitiate was what right did I have to do this to my parents. But you see, I don't know what my unconscious drives were then or even now.

I don't think people are coming here for a refuge, that's a very minor reason. I think it's God implanted in young people. Now when I ask myself if I had it all to do over again, I know I would, because here I can live a life of the mind, I can live the life of extended consciousness.

Not that I couldn't thoroughly enjoy all of the sexual pleasures, and not that I don't recognize that we all terribly need the sense of being loved and the sense of being valued and appreciated—but I also know I don't want to be a housewife. I told my mother I don't see the point of making a bed. There's no evolution—you make the bed every day in the same way and it's the same bed.

My folks aren't particularly religious, but I do think they're holy. In the sense they care about other people, and I've never seen them do a dirty deal to anybody. My dad takes care of so many people, I've seen so many people whose operations he's paid for—for whatever motivation—he's constantly on the give. We didn't have any religion in our home. My dad would always question me. I'd come home from school and repeat something a nun would say and my dad would sit me down and put me through the third degree. So I was always refining what it was I believed in, and the result was that when I entered I never believed in a lot of stuff that I found out later on in life a lot of people really did buy.

We have a lot of complaints now by our young nuns that the structure of the Church has destroyed them. But I can't buy it, because I went to Catholic school, and I'd come home from Sunday mass where they'd tell you if you didn't go to mass you'd burn in hell, and my dad never went to church and we'd argue about it.

A lot of these girls are leaving. They want to get married—and still keep their spiritual side developing. But for us to become secular humanists is not enough. I don't want to go and live in an apartment with a bunch of women. The ones who are leaving point to the structure and say that the structure inhibits them. But I find that the women I admired were never inhibited by the structure. They flew above it.

We are in the process of changing the structure. You see when I went in, I didn't buy the structure. I yelled quite a lot, and they hauled me in and I was told I was a very "critical nun." All I'm trying to say now is that I don't think structure makes people. I think people transcend structure.

When I went into this thing, I never thought about the Pope. I never cared about what the Pope thought. I cared about what I wanted to do with my life. I cared about making vows directly to God. There are these old men ruminating around the halls in Rome, thinking there is a bond between us and them. They don't know it's no longer there. I think there are still some men who have this fantasy that if they came here tomorrow and told us we were excommunicated that we would cry a lot. What we would do is say, Okay, we're not Catholic. In the Middle Ages we'd have been burned at the stake, but they had police then. They have no police now! The only means they have of enforcing their will on us is moral coercion.

There are so many questions. In high school the nuns used to come to me and call me Martin Luther. Now they come to me and say, Cecilia, don't make waves. But these days anybody who takes any kind of a position is making waves.

CHRISTY DARVAS, thirty-seven, married to a successful dentist in the Northwest, and mother of four. Christy works full-time with her community to make the busing program work. She spent the fall organizing house parties between her community and parents in the inner city to meet one another to help pave the way for busing children out to suburban schools and vice versa. She's still optimistic. Her children are beginning to resent all

the time she spends on the telephone, but she hugs them to her and goes on talking.

After I was on television where I came out for mandatory busing, I got all these angry phone calls. This one man called up and said, You know your husband is a professional man, and you could do him a lot of harm talking that way. He didn't go into specifics but it was a vehement kind of threat, like "I've got a lot of friends, and we could interfere with the livelihood of your family." I talked to him for a while. I'm really a chicken and I don't want trouble. It's interesting though, with the wildest people on the right you really can come together if you talk long enough, because they're against a great government thing too.

I was a good kid in high school. I believed in trial marriage and I was never gonna have kids because it was too much responsibility, and I was gonna commit suicide by the time I was thirty. Here I am with four children and not one of them *planned*. I went to Planned Parenthood today and they told me all these things I didn't know. Then I began to think, gee whiz, if I'd known that, I wouldn't have had Peter, or I might not have had Alicia. I wouldn't have known them. The only problem I have with the family is that they hate for me talk on the phone, especially when I'm so involved now with the PTA. One night my husband tried to tear the phone off the wall. (Laughs)

I really love our neighborhood. It's lower middle-class and we have people of all age ranges, and it's not really that high rent. It's a nice place to live, and even these kids who live here are pretty open, I think. The kids really excite me today. They've got guts I didn't have at the same age.

I got so thoroughly turned off by middle-class culture that all I do now is stay home with my husband and children because I enjoy them so much. I went through the *Sunset Magazine* thing of entertaining people I owed things to a couple of years ago and I passed out the other side of that. Then I had coffee for the black parents during the transfer phase of the school thing. I seem to have to do everything that everybody else is doing, and that's not what I want at all. I'm beginning to see what I don't want. I was afraid for a while that I was going to grow old without ever having grown up. But I do think I'm growing up. My expectations are getting more realistic, but I'm not sure that's a good thing. But then I suppose that *is* part of growing up.

What I'm doing is reorienting myself to the things I believed in when I was young and idealistic. I can't throw over what I have here, because it's important to me. I'd like to be a radical, but I don't have the courage. There are things you can do in a limited way. I've done things for the black community, and had cocktail parties, and so on. The best times were when we were first starting. We look back on it now as "the old days" when everyone was working together, and it was really neat and exciting. But the white liberals were so dumb, and the blacks got so hung up on their catharsis and their anger that I don't get involved to such an extent any more.

My husband really makes all the decisions in our family. We try to have family conferences, but usually in any family there has to be an ogre, and he's the ogre. There are a lot of women who use their husbands that way, but I try not to use him as a threat. But sometimes it works out that way. I might let things go too far, or let the kids get out of hand, and then he puts his foot down. He was raised on the work ethic—really, really.

My mother believes in that, but at the same time she was raised in the women's independent thing, so she raised me to think I was going to do something better than work. I was supposed to do SOMETHING with myself, we never knew what, but SOMETHING. I didn't learn to do housework or think about whether I was going to have children. But now I even make Christmas cookies. The kids are really pretty good—they help out in all things.

We give the kids a lot of freedom. My husband (unless he's in a bad mood) and I try not to say no unless there's a good reason. Everybody does what he wants unless it gets in the way of someone else in the family. Like Tom was willing to move to a basement room (we all seem to keep moving around here) if he could have a messy room. So he did and he has. The only thing he has to be neat about is his clothes, because I have to iron them, and it's an infringement on my liberty if he throws his clothes on the floor, which he likes to do. But boys are different. His dad doesn't like to hang up his clothes either.

I was looking at my husband the other day and I realized how very sexy he is. I really dig him. We're wonderful lovers. He's the dominant one in the family, he has strong principles, and even though I may not agree with them, I have to admire the way he lives by his principles. He never approves of things right away, he has to digest things, and then he'll give his okay or he won't—if I get upset, I just go for a drive. But he's the one who encouraged me to get my master's degree. He's all for finishing things and that's good. I've been close to families where the woman is the dominant one, and that can get bad too, sick in fact. I talk a lot with my married lady friends, and that's where you let off steam and complain about your husband, and they say, Oh, yeah, mine's the same way. But my husband and I are taking dancing lessons, we're learning all the dances we didn't have time to learn in high school and college and all my friends are jealous as sin because my husband takes me dancing every week.

When I married him I thought he'd be a good provider. Now when I get mad at him and wonder what I am doing here, I look at him and realize he's sexy.

JULIAN JEFFERSON, thirty-six, has almost given up on having a good marriage. He'd hoped for a closer relationship with his children and his wife. But he's given up fighting, and has thrown himself into his work. He's a research scientist in Texas.

If I were not married, I would dearly love to go off by myself and start something—I'd like to be a lone wolf. But that day is long past as far as what I can realistically do in terms of the family structure. I don't think I'd leave my wife, even if it weren't for the children.

I suppose that maybe one of the things that's led me to believe that marriage is not what it once was, or what the myth led me to believe, is in terms of the emancipation of women. The first six years of our marriage we were very—what I thought was happy. And I suppose it was because she was at home with the children—and I come to find out now that she was *not* very happy during those times. See, as I made more money she was able to finish her degree—and when she finished her degree it gave her a certain sense of independence, and then she got a good job—she was making only a couple of thousand dollars less than I. So it was quite a change. She was providing a lot toward our income, so this independence, and her striking out in various directions, has really created quite a few problems in terms of coming together.

She simply began to assert herself more—whereas before, she was more willing to give in in arguments. Now, there's hardly any compromise at all between us. We just usually bull ahead, because we have to economically—there's still love there, but it's awfully hard to communicate. She has gotten so wrapped up with the idea of money, since she's earning so much with just a bachelor's—she feels I should be doing something to get *rich*! She would very much like extreme, material luxuries —yes! No one dislikes money, I suppose. But it had never been my thought or my aim to have more than just a comfortable living. In terms of my planning, my thinking, my habits, this would require a tremendous readjustment for me to even attempt that sort of thing.

I suppose I'm not really the most domesticated type —you know, family man. She has, right now, all the authority over the children. This was a very strong bone of contention with us, in that I would tend to be harder on them than she. She wants a more permissive attitude. We fought over this so long and so hard that it got to the point where I would be telling them quite forcefully to stop something, and right there and then she would jump on the other side. I decided that wasn't good, so finally I said, Go to it—raise 'em, if they get in my way I'll kick 'em out of my way, but don't bother me with 'em. She doesn't want me to be hard on them, but she admits that she's no good at setting rules for them or enforcing them, and it upsets her greatly if I do.

I think the one thing to do before you get married is to really check out interest areas more fully. I don't mean liking the same sports—that's too shallow. My interests are now so deeply into research, I would enjoy just setting up a lab with some interested people and staying for a while—maybe not forever, but I think I would, I know my wife never would, you see? Her idea of a lot of fun is going to a party and sitting down with a cocktail and talking. I like that too, from time to time, but I want something more meaningful, something more active. I'm very competitive, I enjoy playing games. As a matter of fact I have to drag her to get her to play, to do something besides just talk for a while. If I were looking for someone to marry today, I would look for someone in science. But of course, at the time I got married, I didn't realize I would get so deeply into it. We got married while I was still in service, and I hadn't even decided on my course of study. I think we got married too young.

I guess we'll stay together forever, but if we continue to grow apart the way we have for the last three years, probably not. I think she recognizes this too. There is enough feeling between the two of us that we've always managed to get back together, but we both realize that there is a basic difference in interests and goals.

As for fidelity, I think it's important if one of the partners thinks it's important. If not, I don't think so. (Laughs) But it's extremely important to my wife, so it becomes important to me. If she did not feel that way, I doubt that I would.

VIRGINIA FRANCES HOUGHTON is black,
and a successful journalist. She covers the national
political scene. She constantly interviews people but
would like to take time out soon to write more at
her leisure. A very good-looking woman of forty, her
voice is a bit harsh with an underlying edge of
rage, but it's compelling, and can be spellbinding.
She owns her apartment and is proud of it.

I prefer to live in a larger world than I find in the homosexual community. I find it extremely small. And not
only small, but repetitive and highly neurotic. I may not
know all the ground rules, but I'm familiar enough with
them so that they're not surprising to me. If I got married, the reason would be for a—a larger world, and less
neurotic behavior with my mate.

When I was in college, I went out with boys. So
what? I was never really involved. I went out with them.
I went to bed with a few, but so what? I was never
involved so I don't feel that I was living in a heterosexual
world.

I—I didn't really like boys. I went out with them
because other girls did it. Because that was the thing to
do. And how do you get to the prom if you don't go out
with a boy?

This one boy, Alan—I sort of had a close relationship
with him. He liked me; I didn't like him. And then there
was a boy named Bobby James that I did like, who was
considerably older. As a kid I sort of screwed around
with him a lot. I didn't know what I was doing, but I did
it because I liked him. He was interested in photography
and he was also a tennis player. I was twelve years old
and just for fun, you know, I'd go to see him in the dark

room and he would say, Let's screw. And I'd say, Why not? It didn't mean anything to me. It couldn't hurt me, and it was a—a kind of closeness. And I think I really thought I was an extension of him. I was really a boy. So it didn't bother me, then, being on the bottom, which bothered me later in sex with men.

I don't like being on the bottom. I was a great camp athlete. I could beat everyone playing tennis, and I could run faster than anyone. I could ride a horse as well as everyone. And so in camp, I became sort of the camp hero.

Camp was great. And girls even fought over me.

There was one girl who sort of broke me into it all. A girl from Chicago. She knew what she was doing, but I didn't know. She was about six years older. Which made her nineteen. She was going out with boys, too. But she liked girls. She got me one night in her own cabin, in her own bed. She was a beauty, and she was a great horseback rider. She was . . . almost as tall as me. Dark, quiet, mysterious. All the things that have always attracted me that shouldn't. I know now. There's no real mystery at all, you see. But she attracted me a great deal. So we would sneak out of the cabin at night and go down to the lake and take out a canoe. Or we'd lie in the grass. It was beautiful. Or we'd go up on the tennis court and neck. And I didn't know anything but just—just to kiss. And she finally kissed me first. I was too scared. I'm very bashful, so I was scared. I've always been very bashful. Not once things get started, but initially I am. And so she really started it, then we went home. And I didn't come back until I was fifteen or sixteen, and we bumped together again. We wrote great, passionate love letters in between to each other.

I've never had a relationship with a man where I've

slept with him constantly. I tend to push men away. I haven't even gotten to that in my analysis yet. I just don't like being on the bottom; I don't like, particularly, being aggressed toward, particularly, by men. If it's women, it's something else. But even there, it has to be feminine.

I've lived with the present one for three years. She's unfortunately not as mature in some ways as I am.

But I like a great many things about her. I like her potential, and I—I tried to help and—that breeds its own problems, love and resentment, you know, when you try to help somebody. I was very much in love, and wanted to make a home for her. Well, it's on the verge of breaking up. Yeah, she has to find out who she is now. To do that, she has to go it alone. And I—I have to find out—I have to find someone who's really more satisfying to me. And who can give me what I need. So far for three years, I've given her what she needs. I need an equal relationship. And she's not capable of that, as yet. She's a kid. But, I must say, she possesses a great many characteristics which I like, but it's going to take too long. I can't devote too much time to this. I'm forty.

My family saw my homosexual tendencies very early. My father always disliked them intensely, although he never mentioned them, he was too much of a gentleman. He would never bring up a thing like that. He liked women, himself, and that's why he lost all his money— chasing women. But the subject was never brought up. My mother was an infantile type who gave my father a hard time. Oh, she nagged him, and she was an aloof woman, a withholding woman. I see the tendency in myself to choose these types. I equate myself with my father, and she's the type of a woman I've always gone after. Unfortunately, now I see this, at this old age. Damn it! It doesn't work, no matter how attractive they are and mysterious and exciting and enchanting. It doesn't work. Not for me. I need someone to show something. I don't want someone who's going to hold it back. If they hold back, I don't like it. I get angry at them after a while. I get very angry. On the other hand, I don't want someone who shows too much. It's—it's a very delicate—not too much and, for God's sake, not too little. I mean, that can kill me!

I work with men, and I enjoy talking to them, and I enjoy the freedom of going into places with them. And I like parties where there are men and women. It doesn't mean I don't like parties where there are just women. But I particularly like parties where there are men and women. I don't know whether it's because then I can be a female or what it is. But I just find some men very attractive. I had one male figure in my life, and that was my grandfather. The men I'm attracted to are like my grandfather. They're individuals. I don't like most people because they're not individuals. They don't have the identifying thing that says: I know who I am. I'm me. If they don't have that, they don't interest me. I'm probably harder on men that way than women. I'm much more particular about men.

Sometimes I feel an old-fashioned word called "despair." You know, I feel like what's the point of it all, sometimes. Now, this may be sort of a premenopausal feeling, I don't know—oh, incidentally, I've had a complete hysterectomy, in 1961, so there, again, would be another reason why I don't pursue the idea of marriage. And had this not happened to me, had I not had a complete hysterectomy—that is, the uterus and the ovaries— as my analyst says, no doubt, I might have been—it would have been a plus reason to try to get well to that point. That is, getting well, to change to that point. I can't have children and that would be the number one reason for me to get married. I would like to have children. I would like to have had them. Oh, yes.

I don't think I would want to adopt children now. It's past. But I think it contributes to a certain amount of depression, sometimes, which I've had on and off since 1961. I'm not sure, but women, I think, are perhaps the greater of the two sexes, in terms of potential. Biologically, they're stronger and certainly, emotionally they're stronger. And, intellectually, I think they're just as capable.

CHARLES BENTLY, thirty-two, is an executive with a social service agency in New York. He's had a strong Catholic upbringing. At present he is divorced. He has an infant son, whom he visits every week.

The greatest mystery of my young life is why my wife and I split up. When I met her I knew right away: This is why you are twenty-eight years old and you have never gotten married. And this is why you've passed up hundreds of chances. This is what life's all about. My God, how perfect it all is! This is what the poets write about. This is the kind of intensity of feeling . . . on and on and on.

We lived together for a year before we got married. It was a mutual idea, but mainly financial. I just moved into her apartment because I didn't have a dime. She had a tiny job, but I lived off her in a sense. I paid for the food, which didn't come to much, but she paid for everything else. After a year my situation was a little

better, and we got married. I went around pompously
telling all my friends that they should all live together
for a year because after that you had to be sure because
you knew everything about the girl. If you wanted to
get married to a chick after living with her for a year
then that was really all right—especially after living in
a fifty-dollar apartment on MacDougal Street with holes
in the walls and roaches. I felt that I knew every nook
and cranny of her body and mind and vice versa. So we
got married, and a year and a half later we realized it
wasn't working.

I say it's the greatest mystery of my life, because I
don't know why. She doesn't know why. We didn't stop
sleeping together, we just fell apart. We just stopped.
Somewhere along the way the feeling had died and
neither of us noticed it was dying. We still enjoyed each
other's company—as when we first met, as a couple of
high-spirited people who love joking and laughing together, and we still have that. We are, in a certain sense,
great friends. But the love that was there, the real deep
caring, the sense of a future commitment for everything
you do in the present was gone.

There was a time when I told her she was the loveli-
est person imaginable to grow old with. But almost week
by week, month by month we found less pleasure in
each other, less comfort in each other, less concern for
each other. We had been faithful to each other—we
were beyond taking pleasure in doing anything illicit.
We didn't get a big kick out of living together before
marriage like you would if you were sixteen. One day we
were sitting in the living room, and there was one of
those lulls in our conversation that was becoming increas-
ingly more frequent, and she started crying. And I said,
What's the matter? And she said, We should split up.

And I said, Why? She said, You know why. I said,
You're kidding. She said, No, we're not making it any
more. And I said, You know, you're right.

I use the phrase "fell apart" because there didn't
seem to be anybody pushing or pulling. There was no
outside conflict, no money trouble, we were sleeping
together, we had a lovely baby that we both loved. We
went through the whole ritual of clichés about staying
together for the kid, but once we made the admission
that we weren't making it any more, we began to get
very nasty toward each other. The admission must have
unleashed secret repressions, hidden resentments, like,
Do you have to scrape your teeth with your fork every
time you take a bite? And even in bed, Don't chew my
ear! Little things like that.

Life began to get downright impossible for my son,
who began to pick up on all the tension and unpleasant-
ness that was in the air. He began to get nervous and
fearful. It affected areas I hadn't thought about. For
instance, both my wife and I loved having people drop
in at all hours of the day and night, we'd put people up,
have small parties. But when we decided to split I think
we were ashamed of ourselves. We didn't want our
friends to see the tension, so often we wouldn't answer
the door. We didn't want them to see the change in our
lovely relationship. The ones who did come noticed
immediately. They tried to counsel us with all the
clichés, but none of them were true.

We went to the priest who married us for counseling,
but he couldn't tell us anything, because we couldn't
tell him anything. There was nothing specific. He said
that it might just be a temporary setback—for the sake
of the child we should give it a whirl. So we did for a

while. But it got worse. We finally split, and we've remained split.

For a year after we split, I saw no one, and she did the same thing. It's only recently that she's seeing someone. He's at the house often enough that my son refers to him as "uncle."

It's hard for a guy like me, who's got the massive ego that I've got, who's always regarded myself as very perceptive, very sensitive, and very bright, to realize, just on a purely selfish level, that all your perceptions and all your sensitivity have somehow become warped to the point where you could be completely fooled by making a mistake in the most important decision of your life. How the hell did it happen? Everything I had told me it was right to go with this marriage. Then you find out it was wrong. There must have been some organic flaw in the beginning that neither one of us saw. I know all about "love is blind," and "ignore faults," etc. . . . but we *did* live together for a year, and I knew we had faults, we were human beings and we loved each other.

We've never been able to discuss the specifics of why we broke up because she refuses to criticize me in any way. And I can't criticize her because she was and she remains a lovely person. It was a strong thing we had between us, it was an intangible. She didn't like me for the color of my socks. That intangible could never have been described, and now that it's gone, it's certainly no easier to describe.

The only change that happened was I enjoyed much more than I thought possible the idea of being a father. I thought I'd find it a horrible drag—dirty diapers . . . two o'clock feedings. But I didn't mind it, I enjoyed it. It was a revelation.

I made all the major decisions and she enjoyed it, she subtly demanded it. We lived in a lovely neighborhood in Brooklyn Heights, we had a beautiful brownstone, great friends. So from every index that we could judge our marital success by, it was groovy—money in the bank. We were the perfect couple, our friends called us that. I had friends who were trying to convince some chick they were living with to marry them bring the chick to our place where they could sit and watch this perfect marriage. Several couples got married because of us.

I know dozens and dozens of married people, and none of them are happy—some of them are friends with each other, but it isn't what I call a happy marriage. I don't know one couple who are really in tune, really close, really grooving on each other, looking forward to growing old together. I'm sure there are a few, but I haven't uncovered them.

I should be married. I'm what's known in the trade as the marrying kind. If it had not been for the one inexplicable splinter that was missing, everything else about marriage is just marvelous. I love the permanence of it, I love the planning, the decisions, I even love things like budgeting the salary, I love the kids, I love the visits to the family. I mean, I really swing with it. I want more children.

I'm scared, but it's like a path you still have to walk even though it's dark. I still think it's possible to get married and have a beautiful life, to somehow come through the mess. That's not an intellectual judgment, it's just plain old-fashioned optimism.

If I had to make an intellectual judgment, I'd have to say that, intellectually, none of us are gonna be here in ten years. But if we lived by intellectual judgments we'd all either shoot ourselves or stick our heads in the sand. It's an impossible kind of situation for a young person. It's like being caught in the middle of a battle-field. What young people see around them—their lead-ership disgusts them as it should—the direction the country is going disgusts them, as it should. The fact that Richard Nixon is in the White House disgusts them. And there are very few things more disgusting than that. But you still have the human urge to find per-manent nests to reproduce your kind, connect your survival urge with another person and build a family. But I'm gonna try. If I meet the right girl, I'm gonna do the whole thing over again.

ACHI AHAUA is twenty-two and working hard to forge connections to his religion. He wants to lead a joyous life and admires the Hasidic tradition. He is about to leave on a slow tour of the United States to develop his personal identity and to try to live openly and honestly. He is very responsive to people and likes to observe religious holidays in his home with a large group of friends. He has earned his living since college driving a taxi, which gives him enough money for essentials.

When I was fourteen I was very unhappy. I was a fat, obnoxious fourteen-year-old, and I was the one the boys in my scout troup liked to pick on. I had a Jewish thing, I liked being Jewish—I was proud of it. I didn't understand it, but I was a middle-class Jew. The boys beat me up all the time. I was terrified of them.

My father was not a figure I could look up to. I was always looking for something. My father was always a negative aspect in my life. Then my brother-in-law came along, he was a rabbi, my parents liked him. I wanted to do something right for my parents. As far as my father was concerned I've never done anything right for him—ever. He didn't like anything I did. I couldn't understand it. I became Orthodox in an effort to please him, because I saw they liked my brother-in-law who's really conservative—but observant conservative. So I said, I'll become religious and observant. It was really an effort to make my father happy. My whole life had been "You never do anything right."

My parents never told me what was right, except that it was right to make money, and it's just as easy to fall in love with a rich girl. That's it. That's the whole basis of my father's philosophy—that's where it's at. And that's not just a by-the-way, that's like three times a day with the vitamin pill and everything—It's just as easy to marry a rich girl, and You have to go to college and get an education.

From the very beginning in Orthodox Judaism you're taught you're separate, the men from the women. And it's beautiful, in that the woman has her place. First of all to have children—it's the most important thing. If you can't have children it's *the* most valid excuse for divorce. If you can't have children, the wife will find the husband another wife. Like Abraham and Sara. The woman's job is in the home. While the man gets prepared for Sabbath the woman is making dinner. You see it's her job to light candles. The men go to services while the women stay home and light candles and take care of the children. Then the men come home and the food is all ready. They eat. They eat together. It's

not really that separate—not in most modern Orthodox
Judaism.

However, if you were to go to a Hasidic home—
Hasidism is on the borderline of orthodoxy and mysti-
cism—it has its own set of folklore and religious frenzy
—and if you went to a wedding there, there would be
two separate tables—the men and the women, and the
women first serve the men. The men dance together.
The women dance together. The groom sits in the center
with the men, and the bride sits in the center with the
women. Then they put the bride and the groom on
chairs and they pick up the chairs and dance around
them. There's one dance the bride and groom do together, but they never touch, they only hold the handkerchief, and it's called the handkerchief dance.

Sex is only for babies. Never, never, never for pleasure. As a matter of fact, if you get too much pleasure
from sex there's something wrong—sex is for God!

You can only have sex very few days of the month.
A woman has her period—she's unpure. She's very unpure, and it's a big sin to touch her then, even to touch
her arm. She goes to a ritual bath when she has her
period, it's in the bottom of the synagogue. It consists
of a prayer—usually done by the rabbi's wife. It's an
immersing, but it's not like baptism.

It's only recently that I've begun to question my
religion, because I just discovered that I was only doing
it in order to make my father happy. I'm discovering
that it's a lie. He isn't benefiting from my sacrifices, and
furthermore he doesn't like it, he doesn't like it!

My father has a heart condition which he says is my
fault. He says I never did what he wanted me to do. And
here I spent my whole life trying to do just what he did
want me to do. I thought I was doing what he wanted

me to do, and every time I tried to do it he would say, That's wrong! and he would destroy me a little more. He really has—he's really fucked me up.

It's taken me intensive work to combat this. I've been going to psychologists and psychiatrists since I was fourteen, but it's only recently that I've found anyone who makes any sense—and he's black and he's beautiful.

I didn't understand when I was young all the connections between my religious practice and my sexual practice. In the center comes the father and that's the whole thing. Religiously my whole thing was to do what I thought my father wanted me to do, which I thought was a religious thing. I kept going to these guys for six years telling them there's something wrong with me. They'd pat me on the head, and say, Naw naw, and send me home. Listen, I could kill some of my psychiatrists. They didn't believe me. At that time I was still straight and a nice innocent young boy. I went to them, and I said to them, There's something wrong with me and I don't want to be this way. There was this thing inside me that I knew I was sexually aroused by men. All my life this was going on. You see a groovy body and you get a hard-on, something was wrong. Women didn't do this to me, not until I went to Israel, and that wasn't successful. She was just a tramp, and it was terrible and I only did it because all my friends were living with girls.

I didn't know what to do. She was waiting for me and I was waiting for her. I played this game of wine and candles, and we didn't need the candles. And she couldn't wait for me to do something and meanwhile I thought everything was supposed to happen slowly, but I didn't know what to do, and as I look back on it

I think it was sort of adorable, but all she wanted me
to do was take down the sheets—but I didn't know what
to do—I didn't understand. But we finally got there and
it was just terrible.

It got to the point where I just had to make love
to somebody. I kept going to these psychiatrists and
saying to them, Help me, I'm a homosexual and I don't
want to be. They'd say, There's nothing wrong with
you, and send me home. Well, it happened. I went away
to summer school and I made love like an animal with
every boy who wanted it. That's not the way I wanted
it, I believe in love and I want love, but I was glad to
know that I could also let myself feel like an animal. I
had to love people, my body couldn't stand it any more,
I was twenty years old, and I hadn't made love to anybody. It was very perplexing, but I couldn't kid myself
any longer.

One of the things I learned was that human beings
are human *beings.* What I became aware of was liberat-
ing my body as well as my mind, but it was very perplexing because love wasn't involved.

I've been in love with a lot of people, but I've never
been able to make love to the people I've been in love
with. I don't understand that, but I know that's true.
I hope I can get away from that.

Sometimes I become so destructive in a love relationship that I wreck it before lovemaking can come
about. I've finally come to understand what learning to
love yourself means. If I can do that maybe I won't be
so destructive in my love relationships. I don't think I've
accomplished it yet, but I think I understand it.

People keep seeing things that don't exist. All they
want to do is run away or read things into what you're
saying. The paranoia in the world is horrendous, and

all I want to do is have a nice time, a beautiful relationship.

I'd like to get married. I want to get married. I'd get
married today—I'd marry anyone, a girl or a boy. If I
could just meet someone. I wouldn't go through a ceremony—I don't want to go through that, but I'd like to
marry somebody spiritually. I want to have children.
I want to have children. I love my sister's kids. I want
to have children very badly.

**JANE ROSSON, twenty, is from Southern
California and is getting her degree at a large New
England college. She has been a devoted political
activist, carrying a full course load, maintaining a
high grade-point average, and working every
evening and weekend for what she believes. In the
last few months she has begun to question her
activities and how effective group work can really be.
She longs to go back to her first love, the dance. Her
mind races faster than her lips can shape words.**

I hope that the family changes. I believe in having kids,
but it's probably conditioning on my part, because
probably really loving one person and devoting yourself
to one person is really unnatural, but it's probably the
best thing we can do because you know you're really
creating something from that and I don't think most
people give anyway.

Phillip and I have a sensitivity to each other's needs
and we know how to make each other happy. What it is
is like knowing somebody and seeing them and knowing
that you can help them be the best person they can be

and most people can't do that on their own. And it's in a way all related to the political thing—it's sort of like having the same ideal—seeing the potential for people to live together in a system that's much more peaceful and much more sane than we're experiencing now, and it's working very, very hard and being very sensitive to what the needs of that ideal will be and in making it the best thing it can be.

The thing that's really lovely about our relationship is that I always thought I had a great deal to give but I'm finding that somebody's able to respond to that. It's easier to accept love than to give it. It's much easier to be sort of taking all the time but it's very, very difficult, I think, to give.

We still have to be much more honest—but it's a growing thing, you know. Like right now it's really beautiful. I think it's a great deal of honesty. It's being able to be weak in front of somebody and knowing that they'll love you. It's like the whole thing with your family—because you know that you can go and do something really silly, and really weak and really stupid, but they'll love you anyway—if you have a good family.

I don't think I'll get married soon. It's funny because I really can't conceive of myself—I *can*, that's frightening too. Like, he wants to get married very soon. Only it's a question of money and I want to get my degree, I'm very much conditioned in that sense, too, unfortunately. I really have this hangup about needing to feel meaningful, which everybody has, I'm sure. It's not a hangup. What I'm trying to say is—that it's a real drive in me. Before you can get outside of yourself you love yourself a little bit and you're able to get outside of yourself to touch another person. So that's what it's about.

I think you should live with somebody before you marry them, even though I'm sure it's different because I've talked to a lot of my friends that are married, they lived with each other for years before they got married. The whole thing about marriage is so ridiculous anyway. What is it—the government, Nixon—says it's a sin to live together? Nixon? What is this, some priest or something? It's just so insane. People should just live together.

This person I love has a sort of vision of our living in sort of—a commune. It's a whole community of like thousands of people. It's the most incredible thing. I don't know the details but it's this incredible thing—it's a whole community! A whole community of people living together. They're also political, they live in families and things. They've elected their own mayor, and they all do everything for each other. I didn't believe this existed. Phillip told me about this and we're going to go down there. He trusts groups much more than I do and that's interesting too, to see where he could imagine groups of people living together, where I'm really—I don't know. That's why it's hard politically for me because, you know, I can really theorize, I can give you the whole structure, what it should be like, what kind of jobs, where the money should be allocated—but I really don't know whether I believe. I haven't decided that yet. I struggle—like when I'm talking to you twenty different things are coming into my mind and a lot of it in greater depth.

EMILE LANGENDORF. An energetic West Coast business executive in his early forties. Emile is a director of several corporations, a real estate

**developer, a creative businessman who brought
new products into being, and a man who is deeply
concerned with the development of the community
in which he lives. He focuses the same kind of
attention that he gives to his business enterprises
on the development of his three sons. He takes an
active part in directing their studies and patiently
guides them through the process of their education.**

I think the range of common activities in marriages is
greater on the West Coast than on the East Coast.
Parents and the children do more things together. I
think also the variety of what they do is much greater.
People are somewhat conventional back East. Even the
unconventional people are more conventionally unconventional. People are more crowded back East—there
are less facilities to do things. Even in Los Angeles, you
have more beaches, you have more mountains; in San
Francisco, you're only a few hours away from all kinds
of things. Up in Seattle and Portland, you're an hour
away from real wilderness. And that isn't true of the
East.

I think having children is a much greater change
than getting married. The big difference is, first of all,
a loss of mobility. You can't go out at night, you can't
go down to the movies, because there's this little child.
It has to be fed, to be cared for.

And you lose economic mobility. In the same sense
that during the early part of the marriage the wife is
working, the husband is working, so that there's more
money than they really need, or if the wife is not working, there's the security that she always could work
if it became important. I think a child changes the relationship between the husband and wife. I think the wife

becomes more dependent on the husband. Both emotionally and financially. Because he's both the protector and the guardian. The husband feels this and generally responds favorably, and this helps a marriage.

In general, men do not discuss their marriages. There are some who do—I usually do.

There's a crisis that comes to most marriages when the husband gets into the forties. What happens is this: the man of nineteen is a kid, is full of beans, but physically he's mature, and when he's twenty-nine, he's not all that different. Maybe more strong, emotionally and physically, and maybe the fresh gloss is gone, but he's not all that different. When he's thirty-nine, he's considerably different, but he still feels he's nineteen. He's not conscious of the difference. But I think after he gets over forty, a number of things happen. Suddenly he's not nineteen and yet he was nineteen just a year ago. Another thing he realizes is that he's lived *half* his life! This is the sobering part. Up to this point, I think most men feel they are going to live forever.

Another thing is that he's become conscious of the fact that if he's ever going to have any meaning in his life, or do something with his life, he's got to do it now, or soon, or he's not going to be able to do it. It's like the dentist at forty-four who is making a very good living, and he's got a Buick and a Chevy station wagon in his garage and a nice home, and three kids and a nice wife, and all of a sudden at forty-three or forty-four he feels why should he be imprisoned for the rest of his life just because some kid made a decision when he was twenty-two, a kid he doesn't even know any more, because for the last two years he's suddenly no longer that kid, some kid made a decision that an easy way to make a living was putting your hands in people's mouths and pulling teeth. Now at forty-four he doesn't want to put his hands in people's mouths any more, but the consequences of all those earnings are there. There are the happy children, there is the marriage, and he's Daddy, and he's there for the family, for the daughters and the sons and the wife, and all of a sudden—I'm talking about the successful man now—he really doesn't want to be Daddy any more, in that sense, and he wonders a little. He doesn't want to hurt his children or his wife or anybody, but he suddenly realizes that he is imprisoned. He's confined to a life of putting his hands in people's mouths and yanking out teeth.

Some people can go forward, but you see, if he hasn't used his creative efforts, or he hasn't tried something, as he gets older he says, Here I am confined to yanking teeth for the rest of my life so that the next generation can go to college and drive Buicks. This gets him. This put strains on the marriage.

EDDIE BOO, twenty-one and black, was born and raised in Florida. Eddie likes to call himself Boo, a name given him by a beloved relative when he was little. After getting out of the Air Force Eddie decided to go to college. He supports himself by singing in back-up groups for recording stars and works on his art as a jazz singer in jazz workshops around New York. He's convinced that "acid" helped him wake up from a life of "sleepwalking."

If I meet the right person tomorrow, I might get married next week. It's the easiest thing in the world to meet attractive people in New York, but it's the hardest thing in the world to sustain relationships. Everyone's on the move, constantly into new things, meeting new people —you forget people's names, you don't keep in touch. You stay together if you're in school, or working on projects like our jazz workshop—but college too is constantly changing. You're in the college to get a degree, you don't get that attached. You make friends with someone because he may be better in Spanish than you are.

All the girls are looking for husbands. They look at you with this primitive scary look, like if you'll be a good husband or something. And you don't want to get hung up. But, man, they look you inside and out, really check you out. Then you find yourself sizing up a chick —how would she look in the morning, in a bathing suit, with roses in her hair, and you're doing the same thing. You check her out against a list of images. One way of keeping them at a distance is to play the intellectual game, which they fall into, because they think they can hold a conversation with you. You get the competition going and it keeps their minds off marriage.

If I followed through with all the girls I felt attracted to I'd have a big, big harem. It's hard, man, everyone comes on the scene looking their best and they put their best foot forward, and the girls put themselves on display for the men and the men put themselves on display for the women. I'd really love to go to bed with all of them. But you can only go to bed with one at a time. It's a danger—you might find one you could really get along with.

Girls get nosy. They want to know what you're doing, and what your innermost thoughts are. Girls want their men to be more tender. On the campuses now, the girls feel more equal if not superior intellectually to their men. There's more politics going on on that campus than at City Hall. The Women's Liberation, S.D.S., so many organizations it's unbelievable. I think women are more or less fed up with men, the way they go out and try to get things and don't pay them any attention. I think a woman wants a man to be a good provider and still be able to swing, go to parties, to be exciting and as colorful as possible. I think women want to be caressed more. Women don't really want men to be as stiff and hard as they usually have been; I think they want them to be strong, but to be sensitive at the right times.

I've had this thing against authority all my life. It started with my grandmother, she ran the whole show. She still runs it. I didn't exactly defy her directly, but I defied her pedestal—the one she'd put herself on. She's got all her sons within blocks of her, even to this day. She doesn't drive, she calls one, and he drives her wherever she wants to go. Whenever we had to be punished she'd call up her oldest son to come over and punish us. Even though he had eight kids of his own, he'd come over and beat on us. She had four sons, and unbelievable control over them. My uncle hated himself so much that he would take it out on us, I mean he really hurt us. And he hated me a lot because I represented what he could have been, sort of like an intellectual. He had a chance to go to school, but he chose to get married. He always regretted that.

They were always bugging me to stop reading and do some work around the house. When I'd play the piano, everybody would protest my practicing the piano. It was always a war between the piano and the television set.

My father didn't live there and my mother was up

north, he didn't marry her, and so my other uncle who was an alcoholic would come home and take out his anxieties on me when he was drunk. He didn't want me to play the piano either. Every time I'd be just getting off on the piano, he'd come home and terrorize me.

One day in the Air Force I had this tremendous surge of energy, like I got this blast of adrenaline and felt very lively and happy all at once. I started laughing and singing in the office, and my captain, who never did like me because I was the radio announcer for the base and I was black and I didn't follow orders, and I was a rebel without a cause—well, I was singing, and he comes in and says: Airman Boo, will you please cut out the singing because this is a place of business. I felt really rebellious that day because I was having all these good feelings. I didn't want anybody to clamp down on that. I kept singing, I sang louder. He came back and says: Stop singing. So I stopped and waited for about fifteen minutes. Then I walked to the front office and started this whole scene with this German airman who had seniority. I went into a very weird dialogue with him and it scared him. Everybody in the office thought I was tripping out. The captain came in immediately and took me down to the hospital. In his car I really played it up. I said: Let's fly, Captain McCray, can't you take off? What's wrong with your car, can't you fly. He was scared I'd grab the wheel. We got there, and all these officers standing around, and I said: What's happening, man? I didn't say sir or anything and there were even majors there. So this Japanese doctor examines me and they send me to a psychiatric ward for two days. Then they gave me an honorable discharge from the service with GI benefits.

**LESLIE MILLIONAIRE, twenty, has recently
dropped out of a college in the Midwest. Leslie was
born in Asia. Her family is very close and she has
deep respect for her parents. She was looking forward
to school in the States but found the class system in
her prep school shocking and boring. She managed
to endure the high school years, pinning all her
hopes on college, but here again she felt let down.
A brilliant but deeply troubled young woman, she's
on her way back to the Far East to visit her parents.**

I'm beginning to see that I have a drive toward community. . . . But I don't enjoy politics, I don't like to get
excited about things like that. After prep school I went
completely into a fantasy world, and I'm still in it. I want
a one-to-one, deep, subjective, personal relationship.

I transferred to a smaller school after one year at
Northwestern. I found I was getting drunk and sleeping with any truck driver and construction worker I
could find to go to bed with me, and I'd never be able to
enjoy it. So when I got to this smaller school there were
only about forty of us who were alike and we recognized
each other right away. I fell in love with this poet, and
about eight of us lived in this big house, with two other,
married couples, and it all worked out for quite some
time. The reason it did was because we weren't self-
conscious about it. We didn't make any claims. There
was no hassle about scheduling who was going to cook
the eggs. If you wanted to be alone, you could go back
to the dorm.

It was all very nice for about four months, and then
this other couple and my boyfriend and I were getting
into strange, strange things. Sexually we were mixing up

entirely. We'd sleep together, and then I'd sleep with
the other girl, and then he'd sleep with the other guy
and then I'd sleep with the other guy—it got unbearable
after a while because you didn't know where your alli-
ances were. It was like a whose side are you on sort of
thing—even discussing Spinoza—all of a sudden you
find yourself siding with someone you didn't want to
because intellectually you wanted to be somewhere else.
It got to be that you didn't know who the hell you
belonged to, and I wanted to belong to someone.

I fell in love with Daniel because of his eyes. I like
big, intense eyes. He had black curly hair and a mous-
tache, and he took me home and made love to me and
that was the first time I had an orgasm. All those men
I'd slept with before! It was just a complete anger thing
because of everything that had happened before—I'd
say to myself, Well, here you are, Leslie, drunk again—
off to the walls to fuck again.

I never slept with the same man twice. When I met
Daniel, he said, Hi, Leslie, you look like you're waiting
for a train to come in, let's go find it.

I wanted to sleep with him, but I was scared shitless
because I had a feeling I was really going to enjoy it.
He was so special. I loved him when I first met him,
there was no doubt about it. It was beautiful, but we
just couldn't get along. He was much older than me,
twenty-four, he'd already graduated, but it was clear
from the beginning that it wasn't to be forever. Sleeping with him was great, it was fantastic—there it was—
brought my idealism right back again. But only in one
field—sexual.

At the same time I was also lonely, I didn't have any
close girlfriends, but then I absolutely adored Daniel's
friend's girlfriend. She was stunning, five ten, I adored

her body—she was beautiful—thin, thin. I'd been so insecure about my body for years—and she adored my mind, she worshiped my mind. We were taking this aesthetics of art course, and we decided to turn it inward and create art by the way we lived our lives. I already was in love with Daniel, and while we were taking this art course I was falling in love with this chick too. It was very conscious, it was very created, sometimes I think she was the most original idea I ever had. But she was sort of a nothing person—we had a sort of mind-body relationship.

We got into this very complex thing—it was all my initiative. It was my one big thing. This was my artistic creation for that year. I gradually brought it all to fruition, my sense of timing was very good in this kind of thing. I made this whole thing—imagine this gorgeous countryside, cornfields, and sun coming through the trees, and fishing in the afternoon . . . and riding bicycles. The year before it was politics, and this year it was sexual. And all this time I was falling in love with Daniel's best friend's chick. And this super super day, we all went out and got super super drunk on the banks of the Wabash. We were all smashed and sitting around this little fire smoking grass. The two boys, these two beautiful male forms, got up to wrestle each other, both with black moustaches and black curly hair and they're wrestling each other in this half shade. Jane and I are having this whole aesthetic thing watching this. She got up and went into the bushes to go to the john, and she called me later, and I went out there and told her I loved her. This was the big moment. She said, Wow, she was completely head-blown and didn't know what to do.

We came back to the fire and Daniel must have

known, because he took one look at us and said, Let's make this a foursome. We just sat around on the beach hugging each other. We were so totally out of our minds drunk, the kind of drunk you are when everything is just racing, just beautiful. We all went back to the apartment and slept together and that was beautiful, but from then on I got into a lot of strange hangups. What happened was, Daniel was sleeping with me and Bill was sleeping with Janie on the same bed and then Daniel went over to Janie, and then Bill all of a sudden became impotent because he was so jealous of Daniel and Janie, and everything disappeared. The next day I went to sleep with Janie in her house. I wrote her this long letter and delivered it in person and then we went to bed together. It was so fantastic! It was a culmination of everything. I wondered what was around the next corner.

It was a complete head-blow for me, I'd never slept with a girl before, and right after, I got all scared and hung up. I'd thought about it, forbidden fruit and all that I enjoyed thinking about it, forbidden fruit and all that —and I'm the world's biggest masochist. But I kept thinking, What now? What now? There's no continuity.

I don't know if I still believe in marriage—my parents are so great, but I just couldn't stay with Daniel. Every day after school I'd go over there and cook dinner for him, sleep with him, get up at six and go back to the dorm to change clothes for my gym class. It was like beautiful, but we never went through this whole thing of "I love you madly." In the whole time we were together I said it once to him and he said it once to me and it meant a lot. While we were together, we talked about ourselves a lot, but not ourselves in relation to each other. There was a basic understanding underneath it all that we wouldn't spend our lives together. You see he had to go to Canada to become a Canadian citizen to escape the draft. It was a necessary thing.

I was in a state of shock for about two months after he left, but I'm coming out of it. I'm trying to find something intense to get into so I can keep living. I'm afraid I have a destructive tendency in me. I'm willing not to believe that, but so many people have told me that I do. I'm trying to learn to appreciate the little things in life now. I feel I've lived the great relationships. So I go around brushing my teeth in the morning and try to think how happy I am brushing my teeth.

My mother's a complete idealist. I tell her everything, except the bit about Janie. I think that might shock her. I got this letter from her. She's a great woman—she lost her virginity at sixteen. Let me read some of this. She gets into moralist things, but she can laugh about them too:

> I've never changed my mind about the emotional dangers of premarital sex. But I'm not you. If you think that the occasion might arise here, be sure that you have either pills or a diaphragm. The only hospital is Catholic, and while I know they give them to married women whether the bishop likes it or not, I know they're not going to give them to you. I strongly suggest that you be measured for a diaphragm, because I strongly suspect that your plumbing may be erratic enough to make the pill inconvenient. Attractive men, special men for a special girl, are not plentiful any place, let alone here, but one could turn up. Be prepared, and also be prepared to do anything in secret. The foreigners won't know what's happening, but every servant in town will. I'm not supporting any of the above ideas, because they go against all of my beliefs, but I'm ready to assume that I have no right any more to

direct your life except indicate my approval or dis-
approval.

She gets into these verbal things, and she's not really
verbal at all. All she wants to really do is hug me, which
is a good feeling.

**DAVID HARRIS and MARK GOGAL. David is
twenty-seven and teaches school. He works constantly to get closer to his students. He takes courses
in more effective teaching methods whenever he can,
and experiments in his classroom and shares his
findings with other teachers. Mark, twenty-five, is a
copywriter in a fast-paced advertising firm. He is
finding out that he has a lot of creative power and
wants to use it in more significant ways. They are
both involved in satisfying love relationships but are
not ready to take legal steps to marriage.**

DAVID: Marriage and the family . . . it's a beautiful thing.
It's a home—it's real—You're creating a life—which
somebody else is sharing—it's a growth—

I believe in the celebration but it doesn't have
to be with the family. I've made my life different
from my parents'. I mean, my frame of reference to
everything is totally different from theirs. And my
brother now is twenty-one—he's beginning to see
certain things that he didn't see before. Yesterday—
he came over. This is the first visit he's made to me
and my girl. I don't go home. I can't take it any
more. Tension! It was such a beautiful thing to see
the two of them, my brother and my girl. Both of

them were very shy, you know—and they were at either end of the room. She was on a couch and he was on a chair. It took about two or three hours, and then it all started to flow. And my brother was beginning to understand certain things. It's going to take time—but he's beginning to evolve. I just said I moved in with her. And he didn't know what that meant, you know—? He's beginning to see that home doesn't hold meaning for him. Now he's in a void. He's a very nervous kid. I should really help him find his own way.

I met my girl at a meeting. She'd been living on my block for two years, in the next building, and I'd never met her. She's a great person. If we ever get married, it will be great. If it didn't happen, I would be very, very sad. So far it's beautiful, so why marry? I don't want to say anything about it— I want to be able to flow with it. I used to read Bertrand Russell—if you read Bertrand Russell you're very much involved with definitions and structure. You say what does this mean, what does that mean—and you lose the essence of things, because you're always on the perimeter—and then certain things happen. I'm not worried about what the form is—as much as the content.

There were three girls who really struck fire in me before Emily, but we just couldn't live together. The fires were there but they didn't work.

My parents have a sad marriage. It's really sad because they don't laugh—there's no spontaneous laughter. It's a sad thing—as though they're frightened. They're good, but they're frightened. They're about fifty. My father grew up in the Depression, and he really had to know what security was. Nobody could take that away from him, you know. When he talks about it, it's real to him. My life was very easy in a certain way.

We were spoiled. I know I am. I was protected from a lot of things that were going on in the house because they didn't want me to know what the worst things were.

MARK: Why do you think people are still so hung up about sex?

DAVID: Because they're afraid of it.

MARK: If you're free about sex—it's like the one area that you can be free. The one area where people can dream!

DAVID: It's like this. My girl Emily was writing a paper on a child's concept of death. If you read Heidegger and Kierkegaard and all of the existentialists you can find out that death is the confrontation. Death is what everybody's uptight about, not sex. When you understand the concept of death, then you can understand what it is to be alive because it's the exact opposite. Now most people are still hung up about sex.

MARK: Yeah, middle-class Jews! Maybe sex is an area that people can deal with. The guy in college—he deals with it by saying, I'm a stud—you know? (Laughter) I don't think that sex is such a fantastically difficult thing to face. I think it's one of the easiest things to face. Sex is screwing and sex is love.

DAVID: One of the greatest lessons I ever taught in my life was in a vocational high school. We had a bull session. I asked what they wanted to talk about. They said, Girls. And I said, Great! But if you can't take it, go to the john. (Laughter) You know, if you can't talk about it without giggling, I'll give you a pass to the john. And the kids evolved this little thing—which I called the trilogy of relationship—for them. There was a meeting of the mind, the soul, and the body. It's the whole idea of love, soul, and the body. It's a thing that's intangible in its numerical value. Each couple finds its own way of bringing it about. But if any one of those things is overemphasized, the whole thing is cut off—it just dies—never works. And these kids came to understand what that means.

MARK: They had no problems?

DAVID: No.

MARK: How many kids in the class?

DAVID: About thirty. There were two faggots. (Laugh) At the beginning, they started to laugh, and then we started talking about the fact that—Hey, what about that girl everybody sleeps with? I don't want her.

MARK: What about the faggots? Did they join in?

DAVID: They joined in. They were very quiet, you know. But it was like they began to understand just how great it was to walk with a girl—how great it was just to hold her hand. The moments of beauty in that.

MARK: What people are really afraid of today is commitment. I acknowledge this—I'm a product of this age. But I'm trying to fight for the fact that I want to make my life a committed life—I want—I want a home!

DAVID: I would like to have a family and kids, but the hardest part of it is the commitment to it. You know —like going out with the family—very nice—I was brought up to that—yes—and it's really a fantastic struggle for me to say to myself, I would be willing to spend my life with this girl.

Why does it become an either/or situation? That is what I don't understand. We pose it in such mathematic terms—it's either/or. It's like, if you commit yourself to another person, your whole life doesn't belong to you any more.

MARK: I don't buy that. I have this great couple who's friends of mine—they are so beautiful—I love these people—I've learned so much just by being friends with them. They're in their mid-forties. They've got so much of a life force—they're so involved—that they just emit life. He does his thing, she does hers. There's a sharing. There is no strain. Then when you have to go into the world again, you go into it differently. My girl came here from Chicago to be close to me. I spend most of my time with her at her apartment.

DAVID: Have you moved in?

MARK: I've only been able to get into that gradually, because it's very hard to give up the position of being the cherished son. I get along fairly well with my parents.

I don't want to leave home—I don't want to leave my mummy and daddy—I don't want to leave my brother. My parents are old leftists—they were fairly hip parents to grow up with. They understand what I'm talking about. I kind of appreciate that. If I move away from that, what do I have? Where can I plant my roots? . . . Can I sink them in Fordham Road? Can I sink them up in Mount Vernon?

I think one of the terrifying things about getting closer to Nancy, you know, and making commitments there, is if I make a commitment to that, then I have to make a commitment to a life-style.

DAVID: Why is the commitment to the family first? Why isn't it a commitment to yourself?

MARK: Well, it is a commitment to myself.

DAVID: No, it's a commitment to Nancy first. Then you say your life-style.

MARK: Yes, I'm saying I'm afraid of that. I'm afraid of making that commitment.

DAVID: To yourself first, and then to Nancy? Or to Nancy first?

MARK: No, it's myself, my life-style. Her whole life-style is secondary to *my* life-style. I think it's a human feeling. But it's a terrifying thing to say—you know, being kind of in a position of being a student. If I were to move away from my family—you know, be my own man, make my own life-style, the way I want it—it's in a sense very frightening.

DAVID: Then you really are family-oriented—and that's what I'm trying to say. You see, because of the tinsel we've become externally oriented and other-oriented. What I'm trying to say is, after five years of teaching, I've learned something. The greatest role I can have as a teacher—the greatest role I can have as a parent—is that I can enable this person to make his own decisions, from a root feeling of himself, and guide the person not into the actual decisions—whether "A" is good or "B" is good—but in the process of his decision-making, so that when the kid does become twenty-one, he doesn't have to be worried about whatever choices are out there because he is dealing from within himself rather than the external framework. The famous "they"—

MARK: There was always the "they"—"*they* wouldn't let me in the game." (Laughs)

DAVID: And this externalization we have—this tinsel—
we've built a whole life of externalizations—we've
never really confronted ourselves. People have this
myth about men, especially girls. Especially older
women. Young girls look up to men incredibly—
they're very idealistic about men, no matter what
they may say to your face when they're talking to
you—they're very idealistic. But older ladies are
very resentful—looking back. . . . They think that
men have power—all the power and position.

MARK: There's a historical validity to that, you know—
there's no getting away from it—but I want to be
in love. I want a close relationship.

DAVID: That bugs me, man, that bugs me! I can't stand
it. That's another bullshit word that goes around.
"Relationship"—what is that? There are certain
essentials that a man must have as well as a woman
—in terms of living, you know—and it's the feeling
of being involved. A man has a sense of belonging
to another human being. And not in a sense of
dominating with his own crazy ego flying around.
The sharing thing. This whole concept of love which
nobody can define and which everybody in some
way understands. You see there are certain things
that I don't give a shit if they aren't defined.

MARK: Well, hopefully in marriage you get something
back from the other person. If you have a good job
you might get something back from that job. . . .
Some people get no pleasure out of their jobs—some
people get no pleasure out of their marriage. To me
a friend is much more than the family is worth today.

DAVID: Yeah.

MARK: You know, a friend is much more, like when I

say Dylan Thomas could be a friend, you know. It implies—

DAVID: You think of him as your friend?

MARK: He's a real friend. It's like saying, okay, Camus was something to me. Eliot is something, you know. These people become fathers. When I talk about being a friend, it encompasses all sorts of things that are the guide through time because I've never met them. To me, you know, my family's going to be created by myself. It's not going to be blood, except my immediate family.

DAVID: What do you mean?

MARK: Well, like I have a relationship with my parents of necessity, in a certain way. That doesn't mean I don't like them or I don't understand certain things. But they're not in my frame of reference, in my real living. I can't share with them because they don't understand and it's useless to try to go out and explain all the time. So, like, my friends have become my family, you know, and this, to me, is more of a family because all the family, to me, means is that they are a group of people who love. And so whatever has to be, they're always there. That's a family. It's not the artificial blood ties.

DAVID: If you're in trouble, do they come around you?

MARK: Oh, my friends—I have one friend that saved my life. I owe him my life.

ELAINE JONES, thirty-two, an executive in a large Midwest corporation. She has a staff of more than fifty people and seems to be in close touch with all

of them, judging by the phone calls she attends to during our interview. She is able to keep many things in her mind at once; she becomes a different person to each person she talks to on the phone and is yet another one to me.

I've been married seven years. I was in love with Jack at the time, and even more so now. But I'm in love with lots of people. Jack's love for people is much deeper than mine and less easily given. I feel more bound to my husband than I do to other people because of what we've been through together, but that's what I think love finally is—what you've been through together.

Nobody else could match that. It would take a long time to match that, because nobody could have gone through what Jack's been through with me. I have more traumas than he has, I'm more demanding than he is. Like the death of my father, for example. My father was the single most important person in the world to me and he still is. I dream about him nightly. He was a great man. A giving man, a loner, intensely political, as I am; he could fight off the world if necessary, as I can, I think. We were very good friends, and I greatly respected him. He was strong, witty, tortured, he recognized other people's humanness. He drank a great deal, fought a great deal, fucked a great deal. He valued irony above all else, but he could be intensely sentimental. Nobody ever came into our store with an empty hand who didn't go away with a full hand. We always cut the bills of the poor people in half, but they wouldn't know this, we would just do it. This is not to say that at times we didn't overcharge the rich. We made out all right.

When Daddy died there was this strange assembly of the very poor and the very rich at his funeral. Our whole family is very strong. All except me have children. I not only have no need, no burning need to have children, I have *minus* need. My husband wants children, but he keeps putting it off to the future, so that I think by the time he's ready, we'll be eighty and dried up, so it's really no problem to me. I might sometime adopt a child, but I'm not sure. It seems to me there's such a terrible overabundance of people that we should all go around begging each other not to have children.

We have lots of friends, his, mine, and ours; most of them seem to be single people. We have lots of freedom, we don't feel the need to live together every minute. It's been like this from the first day we were married. I guess we lived together before we were married about as much as we have since we were married.

I slept around a lot before I was married, but I never played house. Certainly these experiences helped me to grow, but I didn't consider it a means to an end. I didn't go around measuring penises, for instance—they were just pleasurable times. But as for finding the right person, I think if we have any intelligence at all, we gravitate toward those who complement us and those we complement. There comes a time when you want someone around more permanently because you're good friends, they help you, and you desire to form a more permanent bond.

I would say sexually that our marriage is better now than it was when we were first married. Jack's a friend as well as a lover—it's been really good these last two or three years sexually—I'm not sure why, sometimes it isn't. I suppose each year you incorporate a bit more of one another's rhythm, our rhythms seem to mesh now both sexually and in terms of a larger life-style.

Jack and I decided very early that we wouldn't go to

each other's professional functions and parties. We don't do any of that husband and wife role-playing to politically further our careers. I think most of our friends are very envious of our marriage, but they won't admit it. Lately, I'm getting a lot of feedback from our friends. They'd like to try the kind of trust we have; Jack and I both have a great deal of self-reliance.

I don't for two seconds believe that sexual fidelity is necessary for a good marriage. I can't even think of it as an issue. If you have a good lay, you have it, it happens. Certainly I get jealous, but I don't know who I'm jealous of. I have a wide range of feelings. But I don't pin it down, and I don't really investigate it. Jack gets jealous of me, but he can pin it down, he's quicker about knowing who I'm after, when I go after someone, but he never brings it up till about a year later. He's cleverer than I am. I've never confessed, but he always finds out. I read his mail and everything, but I never find anything out about him. He always knows about me, but he never confronts me. He just lets me know from time to time that he knows what's going on with me. Like once a year we have a long philosophical discussion about it. But I think we admit to more than most people are willing to admit to in most marriages. Our marriage is more open than those we see around us. What matters to us is camaraderie, solidarity, being there, going through with it, being a good human being—that's what matters, not this other shit. Sex matters to me if I'm not in the middle of a project. When I'm very busy, I seldom think about it. I don't think it's half so significant as people try to make it. Jack and I fuck a lot. But it's not a big spiritual thing. It's like going to the toilet or brushing your teeth, satisfying physical needs. I don't go away from the bed with a great soulful experience any more than when I have a good bowel movement. You know, I'm satisfied, that's all. If I fuck outside of marriage, it's like going to a Chinese restaurant—it's excitement. Variety in cuisine: variety in cock.

I know that Jack supports me emotionally, but it's impossible for me to see how I could emotionally support anybody, but I'm sure I must or else he'd go and find somebody else. I feel that I take more from him than I give to him. But I don't have the power in our marriage, it's exactly fifty-fifty. When I say that I take more from him, I don't mean I take in the ways that other women do. I don't demand that he be there, or I don't demand that he not go someplace, or I don't prevent him from sampling the local delicacies when he goes off on a business trip. I'm emotionally demanding, I'm possessive, he has to go through certain supportive rituals with me, especially when I'm working on a big project. Also, when I'm around, then I have to be the queen, he has to pay court to me, but if I'm in the next room, I couldn't care less. I'll establish my own court there. We never flirt with other people in front of each other.

I know that I'll live with Jack the rest of my life. When I got married it was really just a try-out affair. Now I'm certain that we fit. My first marriage didn't work out because we didn't have the same goals. It lasted two years. I was twenty-five, and I thought I was a baby. I even thought I was a baby when I married Jack at twenty-eight. I'm still friends with my first husband, and I like him, but he was willing to settle for less in life than Jack and I are. It was just a question of goals.

The great thing in marriage is that I can be as masculine as possible. Women don't have to be so submissive any more, they don't have to be identified by whatever egg happens to pop out—whatever litter is beneath the cunt.

It seems to me that it's a good idea to know who you are, to be able to fight for that. Jack and I fight like cats and dogs, but we have a definite ease in our marriage. However, we did marry late, I think that's good. You've got to live your life. One problem with the kids today, much as I admire them, is that they don't know how to live alone. If I thought Jack couldn't live without me, I couldn't be married to him.

JOHN HAPSBERG, thirty. John has recently begun a whole new life. He changed from working with books and ideas to a job in construction. Until a few months ago, he'd been living in a monogamous relationship with another man; now he's dating women and likes it. He says a work of art helped him to change his life.

I had a domestic arrangement with this fellow up until last fall. I never consciously thought of it as marriage, but it was certainly domestic. I still don't know what was real about it. The way I see it now is not the way I saw the relationship at the time. At the time I embraced it, I wanted it. I thought I was happy, but not the way I understand happiness now. It was the first time I'd lived with anyone outside of college. But the thing was, in *this* arrangement I'd beat the promiscuity racket, which was a very important racket to beat if you're from the middle class. You don't have to go in the bushes or in the park—very important. I was raised a Catholic and I couldn't face being promiscuous.

You know, it may sound very corny, but there are works of art that change your life. I saw *The Concept* at Café La Mama in New York. I saw it twice, and cried. It was the first time I experienced any real feeling or emotion. I mean gut feeling, not mind. Anyway, I went out to Staten Island to meet the people at Daytop who'd made this play. I spent the day there and I was just snowed out of my mind. These people were fantastic—incredible—like a new race of people. It's like they'd drowned, come back, and were much better than anybody else. Somehow in the process of getting straight —coming off heroin—they not only get themselves together but they come out more together than anybody who's never been on drugs. I keep thinking it's like the Phoenician sailor that T. S. Eliot talks about, who drowned but didn't die. It's like you almost have to go through hell to learn to live.

While I was there that day, I heard about an encounter group run by staff members as part of what they call "Outreach"—into the larger community. It began as an educational program for ex-addicts and what they call the "straight" community. I went into it last August and I immediately got confronted about being gay. To Daytop people, being gay is another form of addiction. Habits that you really don't feel right about but haven't found a way to get rid of. A first I thought they were crazy, I felt awful, I was afraid that they weren't going to let me participate, because I wanted to come there so I could get in contact with my feelings. I realized from the play and my contact with these people that I wasn't in touch with my feelings. I felt attacked in a metaphorical sense, but nobody yelled and screamed

at me. There are no therapists in the group, just people
with lots of life experience. Well, I said I'd think about
dating girls. They gave me a pretty convincing argument. Three weeks later, my lover walked out on me.
Well, I went through despair for about five minutes. Then
I went into the group and said, Guess what? Remember
all that stuff I told you about me not being able to date
girls because I thought I'd be unfaithful to my lover if I
did? Well, he left. So they said, You set it up, right?
So I had to think whether in certain ways I had. Gradually, over a period of the next month, I repudiated
various phases of homosexuality. My strength gathered
when I saw that the world wasn't going to collapse if I
changed and stopped identifying as a homosexual. I
hadn't dated any girls in ten years. I was scared to
death when I started, and I'm still scared. But I've done
it. I've made the transition. I've been in bed and everything. I function just fine.

I've got to be what our culture says a man is. No,
that's not it. I want to be what *feels* like a man to *me*.
I've had to call up all the things inside me that make
me want to shelter someone and became a he-man, it's a
little fucked up, but part of this is what I've had to
embrace in order to stop acting like a woman. I want to
be a male person. I want to be a person and to be a male.
I have to cop to the fact that I have balls and a cock.

I used to think of myself as a little boy, a little boy
that some strong man should take care of. But since I
couldn't get that, I became the big little boy who hung
around with weak little boys.

My parents have noticed the change in me, but they
don't know the story, of course. I won't take a girl home
to meet my parents till I'm really together with myself
and the girl, so that the shock of that kind of mixing

won't throw me. Of course, my parents have bugged me about getting married, but they also prevented that kind of thing by not allowing me to build any self-confidence as a child.

As a child, I was never allowed to get mad, I was taught to bottle it up and keep it all inside. It was always, Don't upset your mother! My father still says that.

Last time I was home we got into an argument, and my mother started to cry again, this is the way she manipulates us. My father said, Look, look at what you're doing to your mother. I blew up and I said, FUCK! Stop crying, you bitch! The blood drained from his face. It was the first time my father ever paid any attention to me.

LINDA SHERMAN, late forties, lives in the Midwest. She works with her husband in a family business. She's just finished the exhausting task of "staging" a formal wedding for her youngest daughter. It troubles her that more young people are not getting married.

I don't know how these kids can go around like this. They never get married any more. What have they got? What have they got? They don't have any roots. They don't know who they are.

My grandmother died in my arms. I knew her. I loved her. I was with her. I spent her last days with her. This is what marriage and a family means. If you don't have this, you'll be alone when you're old. My grandmother was on her death bed, and I was there. She was in grave pain and I took her in my arms. My children were there too. They were small, but they were with me. I had my grandmother in my arms. After the pain spasm passed, she began to smile. She wasn't smiling at me. She was seeing something else. You know who she saw? She saw her own parents. She saw them there in heaven, and she broke into this smile, very shy. She saw her own parents standing there before her, and you know what she did? She introduced all her children—she had five children—she introduced her five children to her parents, and then she died. She died in my arms.